How the Piano Works

An Owner's Guide to Piano Tuning & Maintenance

Jason Cassel, MA, RPT

Cover Art

"Steinway Mandala" by Carol Cole

Photos by Anne Saint Peter

This artwork is on display at the Curtis Institute of Music in Philadelphia. The work is 4 feet in diameter and is made from the old action parts of a Steinway grand piano made in 1920. The work made such an impression on me when I first saw it while servicing pianos at the Curtis Institute. I am honored to have received the artist's permission to include it on the cover of this book.

To order prints of "Steinway Mandala" and to see other pieces by Carol Cole, please visit her website at https://www.carolcole.com/ or scan the accompanying QR Code.

To Keith Kopp, my earliest mentor

Thank you for believing in me

Table of Contents

Preface

"What do you do for a living?"

I have a love-hate relationship with this question. On the one hand, as someone who makes their living servicing pianos, I absolutely love what I do and genuinely enjoy talking about it with others. On the other hand, I know that from the moment I answer the question, the small talk has now become piano talk, and there is no turning back.

> *"Really? My mom has this old piano and I was wondering..."*
>
> *"You know, my daughter told me that one of our pedals isn't working and since I'm talking to an expert..."*
>
> *"Woah, I've never heard that one before. How did you get into that?"*

The questions go on and on. Nothing derails a conversation quite like the opportunity to talk to a piano technician about pianos. Of course, you already knew that; that's why you're reading this book. Perhaps you are a piano player, a piano teacher, or simply a piano admirer. Some of you may even be interested in making a career servicing pianos yourself. The reality is, piano technicians are hard to come by, which is why I believe people can't resist the chance to ask their long-held piano questions when they finally meet one. This book is my way of meeting you. What do I do for a living? I am a full-time piano technician.

Go ahead. Ask your questions.

Section 1

How Does the Piano Work?

Question 1

Where Did the Piano Come From?

The piano was invented around 1700 by an Italian man named Bartolomeo Cristofori. This means that in the year 2000 the piano celebrated its three hundredth birthday. That may sound like a long time ago, but the piano is a relative newcomer when it comes to keyboard instruments. The organ was invented in the third century B.C., making it two thousand years old by the time the piano made its debut. The harpsichord was invented in the 1400s, so it had been around for three hundred years.

What was the world like in the 1700s? When the piano was invented, Johann Sebastian Bach was a teenager. He was in his late forties when the piano arrived in Germany in the 1730s. The story goes that while Bach praised some aspects of the tone, he found the higher notes lacking in power and didn't care for the way the keyboard felt to play. Keep in mind that Bach was comparing one of the first drafts of the piano to his experience playing the significantly more refined versions of the organ and harpsichord.

Across the ocean, Benjamin Franklin was born in Boston in 1706. George Washington was born in 1732, one year after Bartolomeo Cristofori passed away; and Alexander Hamilton was born in 1757, one year after Mozart was born. As the century progressed, Beethoven was born in 1770, just six years before the Declaration of Independence was signed. Clearly, by the late 1700s, the foundations were laid for a large-scale musical and political revolution.

What was it about this new musical instrument that made it so revolutionary? The answer is found in the name Cristofori bestowed upon it: the *Gravicembalo col Piano e Forte*. Which roughly translates to "the harpsichord that can play soft and loud." With time, pianos of this era have come to be known as *fortepianos*, or in English, "loud-softs." To better understand the significance of this, it helps to review how the organ and harpsichord function.

Organs produce sound by sending air through pipes. Harpsichords produce sound by plucking a string with a plectrum. Video 1.1 shows a harpsichord string being plucked. In each instrument, the tone (timbre) and volume (dynamics) are controlled by adding or removing the number of pipes or strings being played. Video 1.2 shows harpsichord strings being added and removed. While this allowed for a fairly large tonal and dynamic palette, these instruments generally could not build (or crescendo) from one dynamic level to another. I say "generally" because some builders were experimenting with swell pedals and other devices around this time, but even those innovations didn't allow for the rapid and controlled dynamic flexibility note-to-note that Cristofori's fortepiano allowed.

Video 1.1 (Left) – Harpsichord being played.

Video 1.2 (Right) – Harpsichord strings being added and removed.

And so, with the dawn of the Classical Era of music, a new keyboard instrument took center stage. On the outside, Cristofori's fortepiano looked nearly identical to a harpsichord. On the inside however, was a mechanism designed to move a hammer toward the strings at any speed the performer desired. Simply by pressing a key with more force or less force, the performer could control the volume and intensity of each individual note. That may not sound particularly novel to our modern ears, but this is because we have come to take this incredible design for granted. Think about it: how would your music making be affected if your piano could only play at one volume, regardless of how soft or hard you pressed the key? Imagine living at a time when that was all you ever knew, and then one day, you had the opportunity to sit down at one of those new fortepianos you'd heard so much about. Suddenly, your musical world would never be the same!

We will discuss how this action (i.e. the keys, hammers, and other inner workings) function in Question 3. For now, it is enough to know that this new invention made possible an unprecedented level of control over playing loud, soft, and everything in between.

With time, the fortepiano continued to be developed, and a number of styles and even action designs were introduced. The most important thing for modern pianists to recognize is that the instruments available to Mozart, Beethoven and even Chopin and many of the other Romantic composers were remarkably different from the piano we know and love today: they had fewer notes, the hammers were smaller, the strings were thinner, and on the earlier models, the "pedals" were often underneath the keyboard and pressed upward with the performer's knees. The Metropolitan Museum in New York owns the oldest Cristofori piano that still exists (Figure 1.1) and Video 1.3 shows the hammers and what the instrument sounds like.

Figure 1.1 – 1720 Cristofori fortepiano at the Metropolitan Museum in New York City. This file is made available under the Creative Commons CC0 1.0 Universal Public Domain Dedication.

Video 1.3 – Hear the world's oldest piano at the Metropolitan Museum.

As the demands of composers and performers increased, the instrument began to align more closely with the pianos of today. At the same time however, other pianos were designed to accommodate homes and smaller spaces, resulting in square grands, bent-end spinets and even the first upright pianos.

Figure 1.2 – 19th century square piano at the Metropolitan Museum in New York City. This file is made available under the Creative Commons CC0 1.0 Universal Public Domain Dedication.

14

As the Industrial Revolution reached its peak, the introduction of the cast iron plate (more on this soon) allowed for the piano to be strung with more tension, resulting in more strings and larger hammers. Thus, the modern piano was born. While innovations continue to be made by piano manufacturers around the world, the grand piano has been more or less standardized since the early 1900s.

Figure 1.3 (Left) & **Figure 1.4** (Right) – Steinway concert grand in the North Ensemble Room of Brigham Young University.

Today, there are only two main types of acoustic pianos being manufactured: grand pianos (with their strings running parallel to the ground) and upright pianos (with their strings running perpendicular to the ground). While grand pianos no longer come in different shapes, they still come in different sizes. Many people want to know if their piano is a "baby grand" or a "parlor grand." The problem is, there really isn't a hard and fast rule for what any of that means. These expressions are perhaps best understood as marketing terms, and not as technical definitions.

Even still, grand pianos could be grouped roughly into one of three length categories:

1. Grand pianos under 6' long.
   - These pianos make up the majority of the in-home market.
2. Grand pianos between 6-7' long.
   - These would be more common in teaching studios, institutions, recording studios, or in the homes of more serious players.
3. Grand pianos that are around 9' long.
   - These would be considered "concert grands" and are most commonly found in performance venues.

Upright piano designs took a little longer to become standardized. We will discuss their variations in the buyer's guide included at the end of this book (see Question 20).

In conclusion, Cristofori's fortepiano inspired a musical revolution resulting in the piano of today. Few inventions have had such a lasting impact. The piano has shaped the centuries since its creation and now pianos are found in living rooms, malls, subway stations, concert halls, cruise ships, hotel lobbies and houses of worship. The piano has also come to play a crucial role at every level of music education, from the elementary school choir concert, to the high school jazz band; from the college student's freshman music theory course, to their graduate recital, and every practice room in between.

It is therefore quite remarkable that those who hear, play, perform and even teach the piano often know so little about how their beloved instrument actually works.

Question 2

How Are Pianos Made?

When you think about a piano, you likely don't immediately think about sheep and a forest of trees, but perhaps you should! After all, much of the piano is made of wood and felt. Not only is the majority of the piano made of wood; it's made from different kinds of wood. Did you know that some trees have soft wood while others have hard wood? The trees with leaves that change color in the fall have hard wood (if you want to sound smart, the scientific word for this is deciduous). Think maple trees, oak trees, or most other nut and fruit bearing trees. Hardwoods are most commonly used in the piano action and the body of the piano. Softwoods are found on evergreen trees such as pine or spruce. Spruce wood is most commonly used for the piano soundboard. It is not uncommon for high-end pianos to use wood from more than a half a dozen different types of trees in their piano designs, each carefully selected for its unique properties.

Not only are there different kinds of wood in the piano, but also the thickness of the wood, the orientation of the wood grain, and the moisture content of the wood are all carefully considered when a piano is constructed. That last one is particularly important. Most piano factories have facilities for drying out wood to a desired moisture content before using it in piano construction. Often the wood is left in these drying units for months and sometimes years before it is selected, and the wood is later returned to these drying units at different stages in the manufacturing process.

There was a time when nearly every major US city boasted its own piano factory. Today however, most piano factories are found in Europe and Asia. At this writing, the United States has only three remaining factories. The Steinway & Sons Factory in Queens, which makes a little over one thousand pianos a year. The Mason & Hamlin Factory outside of Boston, which makes less than three hundred pianos per year; and the Charles Walter Factory in Indiana, which produces even less. To put these numbers into perspective, most estimates say that between 20–30,000 acoustic pianos are purchased in the United States each year.

I've had the privilege of visiting both the Steinway & Sons and the Mason & Hamlin factories, and while each manufacturer's process is unique, all pianos contain the following main elements listed below.

The Rim

I hope you'll forgive me for stating the obvious, but trees don't grow in the shape of pianos. So how then do piano manufactures take wood from a tree and bend it into the iconic shape of a grand piano? The answer is a device called a rim press (Figure 2.1).

Figure 2.1 – Rim press from the Mason & Hamlin Factory.

Long pieces of wood are carefully selected. They must be flexible enough to bend, but not break as they are wrapped around the shape of the press and clamped in place. This is an incredible operation to watch. The Steinway & Sons YouTube channel has a video of this procedure (Video 2.1). Take a minute to watch it, you'll be glad you did. When the rim is taken out of the press, long wooden beams are attached to strengthen the rim. While each manufacturer follows a slightly different process, in the end, they all take wood and transform it into the unmistakable shape of the piano.

Figure 2.2 – Rims at the Steinway & Sons Factory.

Video 2.1 – Inside the Steinway Factory: Rim Bending.

The Soundboard

As impressive as the rim of the piano is, musically, it is not very interesting. The next component is the lifeblood of the musical vibrancy of the instrument. The soundboard is the main resonating body of the piano and serves to amplify the sound produced by the strings. This soundboard is made by carefully gluing together pieces of wood (typically spruce), then planing and cutting the wood to the correct thickness and shape (planing is a process used to remove thin layers of wood with a high level of precision). Particular care is given to ensure that the soundboard isn't flat. Instead, it is slightly higher in the center. This gives the soundboard what is called crown, and this crown helps the membrane vibrate more effectively. Think of the shape of a cymbal. Once the thickness and shape are achieved, long straight pieces of wood called ribs are glued to the bottom to strengthen the board.

Figure 2.3 – Soundboards in the Steinway & Sons Factory.

The Bridge

The piano has 88 notes, but only one soundboard. So how do you get the entire soundboard to resonate when you play only one note, or one section of notes? This is the role of the bridge.

The bridge transmits the vibrations of the piano strings into the soundboard. The strings do not touch the soundboard. Instead, they run over the top of the bridge, which is glued as close to the center of the soundboard as possible in order to optimally transfer the energy produced by the strings into the amplifying power of the board. As a string vibrates, it causes the entire bridge to vibrate, which in turn excites the wood of the soundboard, bringing the piano to life. Smaller pianos, like the one in the Figure 2.4, have two bridges – one for the bass strings (low notes) and one for the midrange and treble strings (middle and high notes). Larger pianos, typically those seven feet or longer, have enough room to connect these two bridges, increasing the effectiveness of the energy transfer.

Figure 2.4 – Soundboard with a treble and bass bridge in the Mason & Hamlin Factory.

Later on, before the strings are installed, the bridge will be planed to its correct height and then masterfully chiseled down on each side to allow room for the strings to vibrate freely as they approach the bridge. This process is known as *notching the bridge,* and it is fascinating to watch. Truly, it is an art form in and of itself. I recorded Video 2.2 in a piano technology master class at Florida State University. I find the craftsmanship involved mesmerizing.

Video 2.2 – Bridge notching.

Sorry, I'm getting ahead of myself. The piano is not ready for strings just yet. Let's back up to where the last image left off. The piano has a rim, a soundboard, and bridges.

The Pinblock

The piano has eighty-eight notes. Do you know how many strings it has? It's not eighty-eight. In fact, most of the hammers hit three strings per note, so the total usually ends up being around 250 strings. No wonder it takes an hour or so to tune a piano! Can you imagine if a violin or a guitar had 250 tuning pegs? Even harps only have forty-seven. Speaking of tuning pegs, each piano string has its own tuning pin. Piano tuners raise or lower the pitch of each string by turning these tuning pins with a tuning lever. The question is, what holds those tuning pins in place once they are tuned? The average piano string has around 150 pounds of tension. How can wood be strong enough to hold these tuning pins in place, and at the same time, allow them to be adjusted by the technician?

The solution is called the pinblock. How does it work? Well, it is made by gluing multiple pieces of wood on top of one another, each with its wood grain running in a different direction. In this way, when the tuning pin is inserted, it is being held in place by wood grains contacting it along its length at different angles (Figure 2.5). These grains provide the needed friction to hold the pin in place, while still allowing the pins to be adjusted for tuning. The idea is simple, and surprisingly effective.

Figure 2.5 – A piece of a pinblock next to a tuning pin. Notice the multiple layers of wood.

Once the wood pieces are glued together, the pinblock is then cut and shaped to fit between the piano's rim and along the underside of the cast iron plate. The holes for the tuning pins are then drilled into the pinblock to match the location of the holes for the tuning pins in the cast iron plate (Figure 2.6). I've mentioned the plate twice now, so I think it's time to talk about how the plate plays into all of this.

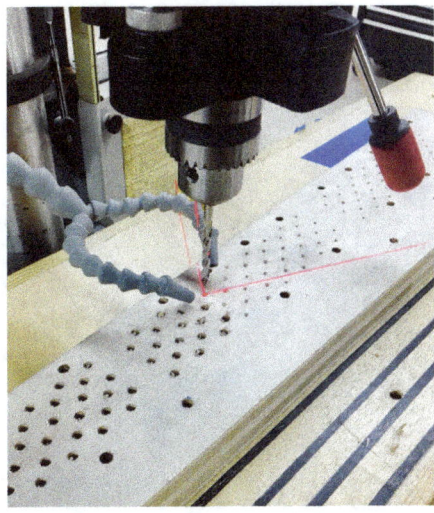

Figure 2.6 – Drilling the holes for the tuning pins into the pinblock.

The Plate

Let's back up for a minute and do some math. The piano has around 250 strings and each string has around 150 pounds of tension. So how much tension is on the entire piano? Multiply those two numbers together and you get 37,500 pounds of tension. That is literally tons of tension (18.75 tons to be exact. 1 ton = 2000 pounds). How does the soundboard not implode on itself? Well, as mentioned in Question 1, it was the introduction of the cast iron plate that led to the near standardization of the modern piano. This plate takes the bulk of the load and allows the piano to have more strings under more tension, thus producing more sound.

Figure 2.7 – Cast iron plates at the Mason & Hamlin Factory.

The plate of the piano is typically cast at a foundry that is off-site from the piano factory itself. Each piano size requires its own unique plate casting. Once the rim, soundboard, bridge and pinblock are in place, the plate can be hoisted up and carefully lowered into the piano. Once the bridge is notched and the plate is attached, the piano is finally ready for its strings.

The Strings

As mentioned, there are usually around 250 strings in a piano. These strings are coiled around each tuning pin before the pin is inserted into the pinblock (labeled 1 in Figure 2.8). The string then makes its way through a piece called an agraffe or under the capo bar, which is also called the pressure bar or V-bar (Labeled 2. The agraffes are circled to the left of the number 2). From there, the string heads toward the bridge. It runs between two pins on the bridge (labeled 3), then around another pin on the plate (labeled 4) before making its way back across the bridge, through the agraffe or under the capo bar, where it is then coiled around another tuning pin in the pinblock. Here is a video of the stringing process from the Steinway & Sons YouTube Channel (Video 2.3).

Figure 2.8 – Tuning pins (1), agraffes (circled) or capo bar (2), bridge (3), pins on the plate (4).

Video 2.3 – Inside the Steinway Factory: Stringing.

The main vibrating section of the string, called the speaking length, is between the termination points of the agraffe or capo bar, and the first bridge pin. The other two sections of the string's length are called the front and back duplex. In the higher sections of the piano, these duplexes are allowed to vibrate sympathetically to provide a fuller sound. Sympathetic vibration is a fun acoustical property. It means that as one string vibrates, another string will start to vibrate at that same frequency, even though that second string was never played. This means that as the speaking length of a piano string starts to vibrate, the front and back duplexes will join in. No invitation needed; it's just how sound works. Here is a short YouTube video (Video 2.4) demonstrating this with tuning forks.

Video 2.4 – Tuning fork resonance experiment.

There are two different kinds of strings used in the piano. The middle and treble (higher) notes use a plain steel wire, and the bass (lower) notes use a wound copper wire with a steel core (Figure 2.9). The plain wire section is where each note has three strings. In the bass section, the lowest notes have only one big, wide string. Then moving a little higher, two wound strings, and finally on most concert grands, three wound strings. I should also mention that as the notes get higher, the strings get thinner and are under more tension.

Figure 2.9 – Types of strings. Wound copper wire on the left. Plain steel wire on the right.

To play a low pitch, you need mass. That mass can be created by either increasing thickness or length. A thicker string has a harder time vibrating. Therefore, an ideal bass note would have a thinner string that is longer. This is possible on a large grand piano, but on a smaller grand (or an upright piano) there isn't enough room for longer strings, so the bottom notes have strings that are quite thick. This is one reason why the bass notes of a concert grand have a clarity that is missing on those of a smaller piano.

Unlike guitars, violins and other instruments with strings, the strings of a piano are typically not replaced unless an individual string breaks, or the piano is being rebuilt.

The Action & Hammers

The piano action contains the moving parts of the piano. These include the key, the hammer, the damper, and the wippen. We will spend a fair amount of time with these terms in Question 3, so we won't linger on them here for long. While some piano brands make their own action parts, it is not uncommon for a factory to have these components supplied to them from a company that specializes in manufacturing action parts.

One area that I find particularly interesting is how piano hammers are designed. We've talked a lot about wood, but what about sheep? While there are pieces of felt throughout the piano action, the most critical area is the hammer itself. The felt used for piano hammers comes from sheep. The wool is treated, pressed, and then glued to the wood core of the hammer using a special clamp (Figure 2.10). Once the glue has dried, the hammers are then individually cut (Figure 2.11).

Figure 2.10 – Gluing the felt of the hammer to the wood core. Photo courtesy of Louis Renner GmbH and Renner USA. For more information, please visit www.rennerusa.com.

Figure 2.11 – Cutting the hammers. Photo courtesy of Louis Renner GmbH and Renner USA. For more information, please visit www.rennerusa.com.

The felt needs to be soft enough to provide the piano with a mellow, sweet tone at softer dynamics (volumes), and a strident powerful tone at louder dynamics. This is achieved because the hammer felt is designed to flex depending on how hard it strikes the string. Think of a tennis ball being thrown at a wall at different speeds. The felt gets firmer the more it is compressed. The harder a key is pressed, the faster the hammer will travel, and the firmer the felt will become upon impact. This is why the piano's timbre (tone color) changes along with its volume as different dynamic levels are played.

Some manufacturers are starting to incorporate action parts made from a composite material instead of wood, there are even a few carbon fiber soundboards out there. No one seems to be experimenting with replacing hammers with any material other than felt. So here's to you sheep, the unsung heroes of the piano's rich tone!

To wrap things up, another common question I hear is: "why are pianos so expensive?" Hopefully understanding a little bit more about how the piano is made helps to explain why.

Question 3

How Does the Piano Action Work?

Very few pianists have any concept of what is happening behind the scenes when they play a note on a piano. They press a key and the piano makes the sound. It's as simple as that, isn't it? Well, not quite.

There are over 1000 moving parts in a piano action with over a dozen within a single key. For now, it is enough to know that there are four main components in the piano action. These are:

1. The key
2. The hammer
3. The damper
4. The wippen (sometimes spelled *whippen*)

The Key

Let's examine each component, starting with the key. The key is the part of the piano that people are most familiar with. The image of black and white piano keys is all but synonymous with music making.

You can find piano keyboards printed on everything from ties and socks to staircases. But what exactly does the piano key do?

The key is a simple lever. You press the front of the key down, and the back of the key moves up. This activates the motion of the rest of the piano action. The key pivots on a pin attached to a wooden rail in the middle of the keyboard. The front of the key also runs up and down on a pin, as shown in Video 3.1.

Video 3.1 – Key movement.

The key on the bottom of Figure 3.1 is from a grand piano. The key on the top is from an upright piano. The back of the key contains a wooden or brass piece called a capstan (indicated with the red arrows). This piece communicates the key movement to the wippen. File that away for now. We will come back to it soon.

Figure 3.1 – Piano keys. Red arrows point to the capstans.

The Hammer

The next part of the piano people are more familiar with is the hammer. This is what strikes the strings to make the sound. The hammer is made of felt with a wood molding in the center. On a grand piano, there is a piece called the knuckle (indicated by the bottom red arrow in Figure 3.2). On an upright piano, the bottom of the hammer assembly is called the hammer butt (indicated by the top red arrow). These two pieces will come into play later. For now, watch Video 3.2 and simply notice that the key does not contact the hammer at all. Clearly, we are missing an important connecting piece. In this video (Video 3.2) and the next video (Video 3.3), I propped the hammer of the grand piano action model up to stop it from falling and to simulate approximately where it would be when all the pieces are in place.

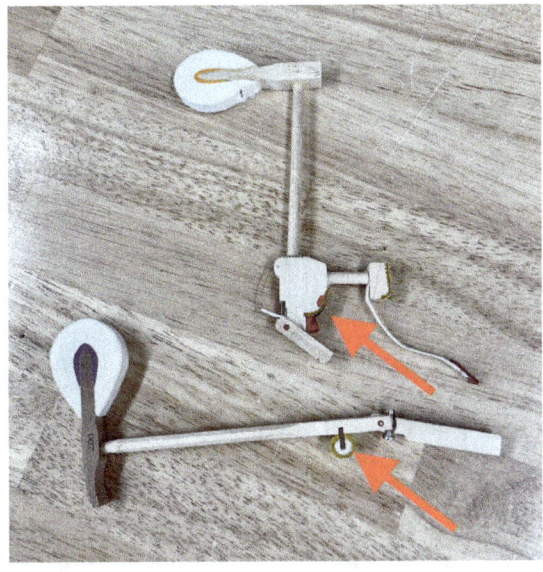

Video 3.2 – Key and
hammer only.

Figure 3.2 – Piano Hammers. Red arrows point at the knuckle (grand) and the
hammer butt (upright).

The Damper

The dampers serve the important role of muting the strings when they
are not in use and stopping the strings from vibrating after the key is
released. The dampers can be lifted off of the strings in two ways. The
first is by the action, and the second is by the pedals. We will talk more
about pedals in Question 5. We will focus here on how the damper is
engaged by the action. In Figure 3.3, the damper on the left is from a
grand piano, and the damper on the right is from an upright piano.
Watch Video 3.3 and notice that in a grand piano, the back of the key
lifts the damper. In the upright piano, we are still missing the
connecting piece.

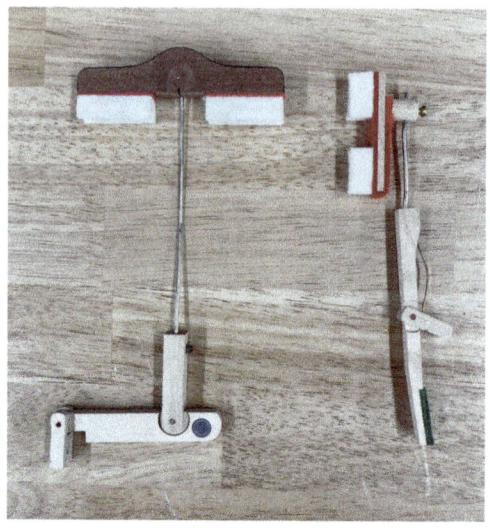

Figure 3.3 (Left) – Dampers. Grand damper on the left. Upright damper on the right.

One question I hear often is, "Why are there no dampers on the strings in the very top section of the piano?" Some people even think their piano is broken or missing those pieces. Fear not; this is by design. The sound produced by those top strings dies out so quickly that they don't need dampers. Instead, those strings are left free to vibrate sympathetically with the rest of the piano.

Video 3.3 – Key, hammer & damper only.

The Wippen

While everyone is familiar with the keys of the piano, and most people have an idea of what the hammers and dampers do, I can all but guarantee that you have never heard of the wippen. Even still, by now I hope you realize the important role this piece has in connecting the key movement to the rest of the action. Without it, the action simply cannot function. Without it, the piano is not a piano.

The wippen on the top of Figure 3.4 is from an upright piano. The wippen on the bottom of the image is from a grand piano.

While the etymology of the word as it relates to pianos appears to be unknown, in German, wippen means "to rock" or "to seesaw," which seems appropriate as the wippen rocks back and forth as the key is pressed and released. Remember the capstan on the key? It is this capstan that transmits the key movement to the wippen. From there, the jack (on the wippen) engages the hammer. Additionally, in an upright piano, the spoon on the wippen engages the damper (indicated by the yellow arrow in Figure 3.4).

Figure 3.4 (Above) – Upright wippen above. Grand wippen below. Red arrows point to the jacks. Yellow arrow on the upright wippen points to the spoon.

Perhaps the most important part of the wippen is the jack (indicated by the red arrows in Figure 3.4). This is what truly allows the piano to play *forte* and *piano* as Cristofori envisioned. The jack rotates and as it does so, it pushes the hammer toward the string. Then, at the last second, the jack gets out of the way and lets all of the built-up energy move the hammer the last few millimeters. A small amount of energy results in a softer sound. A large amount of energy results in a louder sound. This phenomenon of "getting out of the way at the last second" is called escapement.

To understand how this works, we need to examine the jack more closely. Notice that the jack has a "toe" (indicated by the red arrows in Figures 3.5 and 3.6) and at the appropriate time in the jack's movement that toe contacts a button (indicated by the yellow arrows in Figures 3.5 and 3.6) which causes the jack to swing out from underneath the knuckle of a grand piano, or the hammer butt of an upright piano.

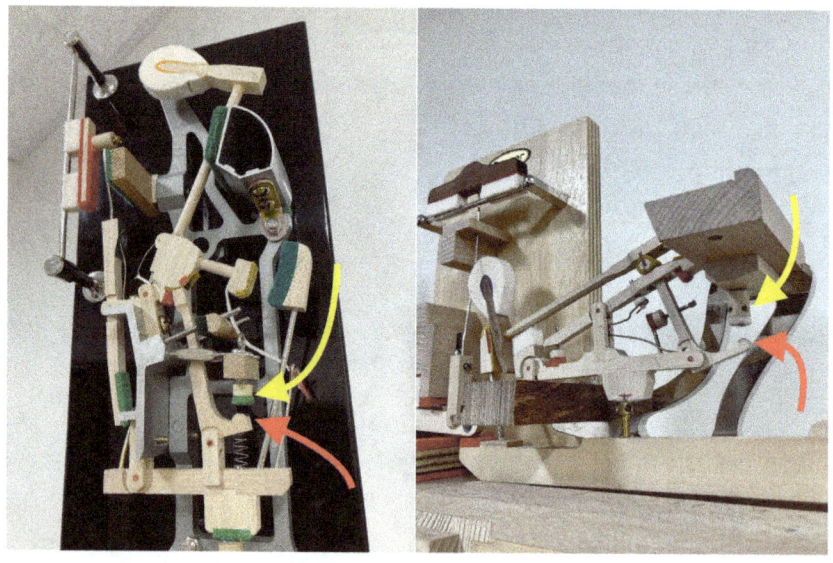

Figure 3.5 (Left) & **Figure 3.6** (Right) – How escapement works. The red arrows point at the jack toes. The yellow arrows point at the buttons. When those two pieces touch, it starts to move the jack out from underneath the hammer assembly.

Video 3.4 – How escapement works.

After the hammer strikes the string, it is caught by the backcheck (located on the back of the key on a grand piano, and on the wippen of an upright piano. Indicated by the red arrows in Figure 3.7). This holds the hammer closer to the string to allow for a more rapid repetition of the next note if desired.

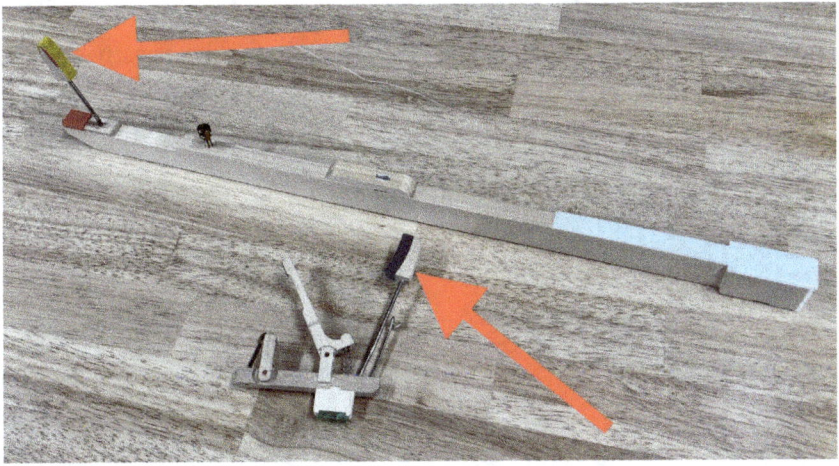

Figure 3.7 – Backchecks. Grand above. Upright below.

While there are a fair amount of videos out there explaining how a piano action works, one of my personal favorites was produced by the YouTuber Mark Rober (Video 3.5). Because of his popularity, at the time of this writing, his video is only two years old and has over 35 million views. That averages to around 50,000 views per day! It is exciting to me to think that so many people have seen this simple and approachable presentation. Like all of Mark Rober's content, the entire video is entertaining and informative; however, the part that relates to the topic at hand runs from 1:23–4:18.

Video 3.5 – YouTuber Mark Rober on how a piano works.

Since understanding how the piano action functions is so critical, here is one more video (Video 3.6) that breaks down the keystroke of a grand piano step-by-step in slow motion. Watch it a few times. It's a lot to take in!

Video 3.6 – Grand keystroke step-by-step.

The Keystroke Step-by-Step	
GRAND	**UPRIGHT**
Step 1: The player presses a key.	Step 1: The player presses a key.
Step 2: The capstan starts to lift the wippen causing the jack to contact the hammer knuckle, moving the hammer toward the string.	Step 2: The capstan starts to lift the wippen causing the jack to contact the hammer butt, moving the hammer toward the string.
Step 3: When the hammer is about halfway to the string, the back of the key starts to lift the damper off the strings.	Step 3: When the hammer is about halfway to the string, the spoon (on the wippen) starts to lift the damper off the strings.
Step 4: The jack toe contacts the button, causing the jack to no longer contact the hammer knuckle.	Step 4: The jack toe contacts the button, causing the jack to no longer contact the hammer butt.
Step 5: The hammer strikes the strings!	Step 5: The hammer strikes the strings!
Step 6: The hammer rebounds and is caught by the backcheck (on the back of the key).	Step 6: The hammer rebounds and is caught by the backcheck (on the wippen).
Step 7: The key is released by the player.	Step 7: The key is released by the player.
Step 8: The jack quickly returns to its position under the hammer knuckle, ready to play the next note if needed.	Step 8: The jack returns to its position under the hammer butt, ready to play the next note if needed.
Step 9: The damper contacts the strings and starts to dampen them.	Step 9: The damper contacts the strings and starts to dampen them.
Step 10: The key returns to its at-rest position.	Step 10: The key returns to its at-rest position.

Question 4

What Happens after the Hammer hits the String?

Imagine arriving at a friend's home when they announce that they just tied up a thin piece of steel between two points in their living room and they are going to strike it with a hard piece of felt. "You're a musical person," they exclaim, "I can't wait to hear what you think of my new instrument!"

What would you expect this contraption to sound like? Probably not like a piano. But why is that? After all, isn't that all a piano is: a bunch of steel strings tied between two points struck with felt hammers? Well, yes and no. In Question 3, we learned about what happens when a key is pressed, but the hammer striking the string is only part of the story.

To illustrate this, I will pluck a string on a jig used to teach string replacement (Video 4.1). This jig has a tuning pin inserted into pinblock material, an agraffe, bridge pins and a pin on a piece of metal meant to simulate the plate. I will then pluck a string tuned to the same

pitch in the piano. Notice the difference? The jig probably sounds more like your friend's hypothetical contraption. The piano, even plucked, sounds like a piano. So what is the secret ingredient to the piano's rich tone?

Video 4.1 – Plucking a string.

After the hammer hits a string, the string starts to vibrate. These vibrations then move up the string and into the bridge (red arrow in

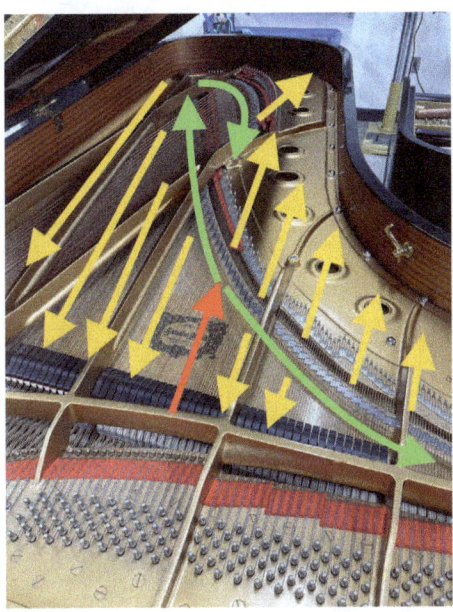

Figure 4.1). The bridge runs the length of the soundboard and so from a single string, the entire bridge can start to reverberate (green arrows in Figure 4.1), which in turn, causes the soundboard to resonate (yellow arrows in Figure 4.1). As long as the string continues to vibrate, it continues to send waves into the bridge and soundboard. The entire belly of the piano is excited and creates a feedback loop of musical resonance.

Figure 4.1 – The piano's musical feedback loop.

Remember, too, that the front and back duplexes of the strings are also free to vibrate sympathetically with the main vibrating section of the wire (called the speaking length). When the sustain pedal is used, all of the dampers are lifted to allow the speaking lengths of all of the strings to vibrate sympathetically with each other, each string exciting the bridge and soundboard even more. Multiply these effects across an entire piece's worth of notes, and the result is nothing short of breathtaking.

While the piano action affords the pianist an astonishing level of control, power, and repetition, it is the belly of the piano (i.e. the strings, bridge and soundboard) that amplifies the pianist's efforts and projects the music throughout the room, or even a concert hall.

Question 5

How do the Pedals Work?

You have ten fingers and there are eighty-eight keys. You have two feet and yet most pianos have only three pedals. If we were to match the ratio of fingers to keys, then there really should be seventeen pedals. Wouldn't that be fun? Yes, you organists have my permission to feel a little smug as you watch your pianist friends squirm at the notion of dealing with that many pedals.

I am always surprised by how little most piano owners understand about the pedals on their beloved instruments. Nearly everyone has some idea of what the right pedal (or sustain pedal) does, but only those who are more serious seem to be familiar with the purpose and function of the other two.

Let's look at each pedal one by one, starting with the simplest, and working our way up to the most confusing.

The Right Pedal (The Sustain Pedal)

This pedal is *by far* the most commonly used. Without it, the piano doesn't feel quite right. You will remember that when a key was played, the damper was lifted by the back of the key in a grand piano, or by the spoon on the wippen in an upright piano. While the key was held down, the damper remained lifted off of the strings, allowing them to vibrate freely. When the key was released, the damper fell back onto the string and dampened the vibrations. This however, is only one way to lift the dampers off of the strings. The second way is with the sustain pedal, which is also called the damper pedal.

Underneath the dampers of a grand piano is a tray. Above the damper spoons in an upright piano is a rod (indicated by the red arrows in Figures 5.1 and 5.2). When you press the front of the sustain pedal down, you lift the back of the pedal up. Attached to the back of this

pedal is a rod that engages the grand damper tray or the upright pedal rod, thus lifting all the dampers off of the strings at the same time (Video 5.1).

Figure 5.1 – Grand damper tray.

Figure 5.2 (Left) – Upright pedal rod.

Video 5.1 – How the grand sustain pedal works.

This pedal allows all the strings to vibrate sympathetically with each other. Remember the tuning fork video from Question 2? Imagine that experiment with a room full of 250 tuning forks. As one string vibrates, it causes others to vibrate. Each string in turn excites the bridge, which causes the soundboard to vibrate. The effect is nothing short of extraordinary. Try this on your own piano. Play a note. Then press the sustain pedal and play the same note again. The difference in the tone is created entirely by the acoustical magic of sympathetic vibrations.

The Left Pedal (The Shift Pedal or The Soft Pedal)

On an upright piano, the left pedal is a soft pedal. On a grand, the left pedal is a shift pedal. Now, you might be thinking, "Wait, aren't those the same thing?" Well, the terms are often used interchangeably, but no, they are not the same thing. A grand piano has a shift pedal, not a soft pedal, and the reasoning for this is found in how the pedal operates.

To truly understand the distinction between a shift pedal and soft pedal, you must first understand how hammers wear with use. Over time, as the hammer is played, it starts to develop grooves in the areas where the hammer strikes the strings (Figure 5.3). These string grooves eventually become slightly harder than the regions in between the string grooves. This means that the tone of the piano will change depending on which area of the hammer strikes the strings.

When you press the left pedal on a grand piano, the back of the pedal rises. Attached to the back of this pedal is a rod that engages a lever that physically shifts the action toward the treble (to the right). This causes the hammers to strike the strings in between the established string grooves. This not only lowers the volume of the piano, but by striking the strings with a different region of the hammer felt, it also alters the tone of the piano. See Figures 5.4 and 5.5, as well as Video 5.2.

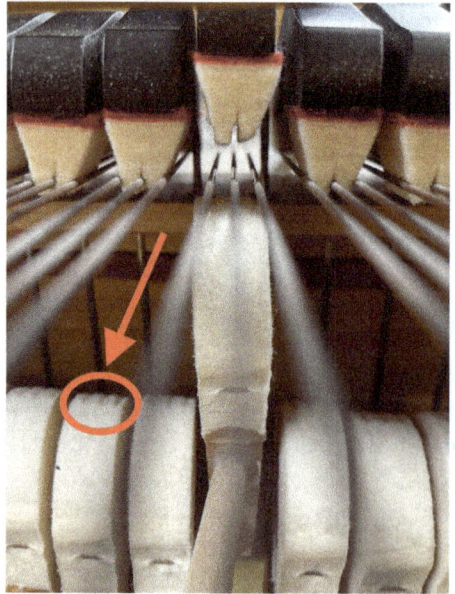

Figure 5.3 – String grooves circled in red.

 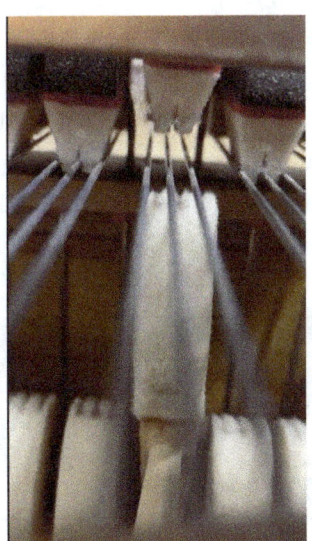

Figure 5.4 (Left) – Before shift. String grooves are in line with the strings.

Figure 5.5 (Right) – After shift. String grooves are no longer in line with the strings.

 **Video 5.2** - Hammers shifting.

At the completion of the pedal's movement, the hammer will only strike the middle and right strings of each note (or the pedal can be adjusted to just barely strike the left string of each note). Fun Fact: Another name for this pedal is the *una corda* pedal, which translates to the "one string" pedal. This is because on early fortepianos, they only had two strings per note, and so the shift pedal caused the action to shift and only play one string per note. Technically, on a modern piano we should refer to this pedal as the *due corde* pedal, but something tells me that name isn't likely to catch on.

When the shift pedal is released, a return spring attached to the treble side of the piano pushes the action back to its original location. This return spring is indicated by the larger red circle in Figure 5.6. The smaller red circle shows the top of the shift lever, which pushes the action toward the treble. Watch Video 5.3 to get a clearer sense of this entire process.

Figure 5.6 – Shift lever and return spring.

Video 5.3 – How the shift pedal works.

Now, let's examine the soft pedal of an upright piano. In this system, when the left pedal is pressed, the hammers are pushed closer to the strings. By reducing the distance the hammers travel before striking the strings, the potential energy is limited and so is the volume. The sound is now softer; but tonally, it remains the same. This is because the hammers are still striking the strings in the hammer grooves. See Figures 5.7 and 5.8, as well as Video 5.4.

Figure 5.7 (Left) – Before soft pedal. Hammers are farther from the strings.

Figure 5.8 (Right) – After soft pedal. Hammers are closer to the strings.

 **Video 5.4** – Soft pedal in use.

So yes, a shift pedal is not the same as a soft pedal. In fact, the shift pedal on a grand piano might more accurately be called a timbre pedal than a soft pedal. The difference between the two systems is so pronounced that some brands, most famously Fazioli in Italy, feature a fourth pedal. This fourth pedal is a true soft pedal that reduces the volume *without* changing the timbre, offering the pianist the choice between the standard shift pedal, a soft pedal, and even a combination of the two. These fourth pedal systems are particularly advanced because they not only raise the hammers closer to the strings, but also lower the keys to limit their travel as well. This maintains the touch of the piano far better than the standard upright soft pedal system that only reduces the hammer travel without compensating for this in the keys. Video 5.5 shows how the hammers behave as the shift pedal and fourth pedal are used. It also shows the keys lowering when the fourth pedal is pressed.

Video 5.5 – Fazioli shift pedal and fourth pedal in use.

The Middle Pedal (the Sostenuto Pedal, Bass Sustain, or Upright Practice Pedal)

Finally, we have arrived at the least used and least understood feature in the entire piano: the middle pedal. Part of what makes this pedal so nebulous is that it can do different things on different pianos; but even when the middle pedal functions as a sostenuto pedal (which could be considered the standard), there are very few people who actually understand how the pedal is supposed to work. We will begin by examining the standard sostenuto pedal. We will then discuss some of the alternative functions you might come across in other pianos.

Sostenuto is Italian for "supported." At the moment, this translation likely doesn't help much. So let's dive in and hopefully things will start to fall into place. Remember that there are two ways to lift the dampers in the piano. The first is by pressing a key. When a key is pressed, the damper is lifted by either the back of the key on a grand piano, or the spoon attached to the wippen of an upright piano. The second method is to lift all of the dampers simultaneously with the sustain pedal (a.k.a. the right pedal) which lifts the damper tray in a grand piano, or rotates the damper rod in an upright piano.

In other words, a single damper can be lifted as long as its key is held down by the player, and all of the dampers can be lifted by the sustain pedal. But what if the pianist wanted another option? For example, what if the pianist wanted the dampers of two notes in the bass to remain lifted while both hands were available to play a staccato passage in the treble? (Staccato means "detached," meaning that the duration of the notes is short and not sustained.)

This imaginative option is made possible by the sostenuto pedal. When the sostenuto pedal is pressed, it "supports" (or holds up) only the dampers that were lifted when the pedal was pressed. So if a low C was played in the bass, and the middle pedal was pressed, then only the damper for that low C would be held up. All other dampers would remain in contact with the strings. When another note is played, then the damper for that note would be lifted only as long as the note was held down. When that note was released, its damper would fall and dampen the string. Meanwhile, that low C is still allowed to sustain and vibrate sympathetically as long as the middle pedal is pressed down. Pretty neat, right?

If that explanation didn't make sense, then watch Video 5.6. Even if it did make sense, you should still watch it. I should also mention that while this video holds up dampers in the bass of the piano, any damper can be held up with the sostenuto pedal, not just those in the bass.

Video 5.6 – Sostenuto pedal in use.

So how does this work? Well, let's look closer at the damper of a grand piano. The damper tray and the back of the key hold the dampers up by pressing up on the bottom of the piece that holds the damper wire. Notice the small red tab attached to this piece? (Figure 5.9) That is called the damper tab and it is important.

Figure 5.9 – Damper tabs.

In addition to that little red tab, the piano also has a rail called the sostenuto rail that rotates when the middle pedal is pressed. If a damper is lifted when the middle pedal is pressed, then the sostenuto rod will hold up the damper tab for that damper.

When the sostenuto rod is rotated like this, the damper tabs of the other notes are pushed down when they contact the rod. This prevents them from being held up by the sostenuto rod.

When the middle pedal is released, the sostenuto rod rotates back and the damper tab is no longer held up. The damper falls and dampens the strings. If the last two paragraphs were difficult to follow, then watch Video 5.7 and re-read them. If a picture is worth a thousand words, then it stands to reason that a video must be worth thousands.

Video 5.7 – How the sostenuto pedal works. At the beginning of this video, you can see the dampers at the top (above the strings). Throughout the video, I am using my finger to simulate the back of the key lifting the damper.

Now, onto some common alternatives. As you have likely gathered by now, a sostenuto system adds a level of complexity to the design of a piano. Since casual players rarely use it, a true sostenuto pedal is typically only found on nicer grand pianos and on a few high-end uprights. An entry-level grand piano, as well as most upright pianos, would be more likely to include what is called a bass sustain pedal. I call it a "mock sostenuto," because it simulates one of the more common effects of the sostenuto pedal by using a much simpler system. A bass sustain pedal only lifts the dampers in the bass section of the piano. This allows the bass notes to sustain and vibrate sympathetically, while the midrange and treble dampers are still in contact with the strings unless an individual note is played; thus imitating a sostenuto pedal without the need for a sostenuto rod and damper tabs.

The system works by having two damper trays, or two damper lift rods. When the right pedal is pressed, both damper trays are lifted (grand), or both damper lift rods are rotated (upright). When the middle pedal is pressed, only the bass damper tray is lifted (grand), or the bass damper lift rod is rotated (upright). This approach is much simpler and less expensive.

 Video 5.8 demonstrates how this system works on an upright piano. First, you will be shown the dampers lifting off the strings, alternating between the right and middle pedals. Then, with the action removed, I will use my finger to push up on the damper lift rods controlled by the right and middle pedals.

Video 5.8 – Bass sustain on an upright piano.

Another alternative on upright pianos is what is commonly referred to as the practice pedal. These pedals insert a piece of felt in between the hammers and the strings. The result is a significantly quieter and muted sound. The idea behind this pedal is that it can be used when you need to practice but you don't want to bother the people in the neighboring apartment, or you want your kids to practice, but you also don't want a migraine. Often, these pedals can be locked in place by pressing the pedal down and then over to the left. This frees your feet to play the right pedal and left pedal as desired.

Figure 5.10 – Practice pedal felt.

Video 5.9 – Practice pedal in use.

Finally, I should mention that on some older pianos, the middle pedal is simply decorative and actually does nothing other than sit there and look nice, because you know, pianos are supposed to have three pedals, right?

Question 6

How Do I Remove a Pencil from My Piano?

Raise your hand if you've ever dropped a pencil into a grand piano. I know I can't see you, but I'm just going to imagine that if you've ever played a grand piano, then your hand is raised.

While I don't often get service calls about lost pencils, once every couple of years I get a panicked call from someone saying that they dropped their phone into the piano. I assume they must be calling from a spouse's phone? You know, I've never really thought about that until writing this.

I first ask them about the brand of their piano. Then I ask them how brave they are feeling. This usually results in a nervous chuckle. I assure them that I'm serious, and then explain that I will talk them through this process over the phone. Usually, within a few minutes, I hear cheering and rejoicing from a room full of people I didn't even know were there watching the whole time with rapt attention. Now you have this book, so you won't need to call me!

Before we can begin, we must first familiarize ourselves with some terminology. Meet your new friend, the fallboard (labeled 1 in Figure 6.1). The fallboard is the piece of wood that covers the keys of your piano when closed. It also doubles as a slide for pencils, as you have likely discovered. On each side of the keyboard are the cheekblocks (labeled 2). Cute, right? It's like those blocks are the piano's cheeks and the keys are its teeth. Maybe that's what they were going for, but who knows? Anyway, running across the front of the keys is another piece of wood called the keyslip (labeled 3). Stare at the image until these three pieces are ingrained in your memory. I'll be referencing them freely moving forward and I don't want to lose you.

Figure 6.1 – Grand piano case parts: fallboard (1), cheekblocks (2), keyslip (3).

In order to retrieve your pencil (or cell phone) you will need to remove the fallboard. There are two common methods for removing the fallboard: the easy way and the less easy way. Most piano brands follow the easy method, but a handful of brands do not. Fortunately, neither method is beyond you, and all you will ever need is a screwdriver. So, how brave are you feeling?

Method 1: The Easy Way

First, look at the bottom left and bottom right corners of the fallboard. Do you see any screws? If so, you will need to remove those first.

Once the screws are removed, or if there were no screws in the first place, all you need to do to remove the fallboard is simply stand in the middle of the piano, grab the fallboard firmly with your hands and pull straight up. If your piano follows the easy method, then the fallboard should come right out. Gently set the fallboard somewhere safe. It is now time to remove that pencil, paper clip, or whatever else has fallen in.

Getting the fallboard back on is a little trickier. Notice the slots on each side of the piano (Figure 6.2). Now locate the pin or rectangular piece on each side of the fallboard (Figure 6.3). Your job is to insert those pins into those slots. Stand in the center of the piano, hold the fallboard firmly with both hands and align the pins to the slots the best you can. This will likely mean that a section of the fallboard needs to be slightly inside the piano. Once aligned, lower the fallboard evenly so that the pins go in *at the same time*. That last part is important. If one side falls in first, don't try to be a hero, simply pull it out and start over until they both go in together. Once in place, return the two screws (if applicable).

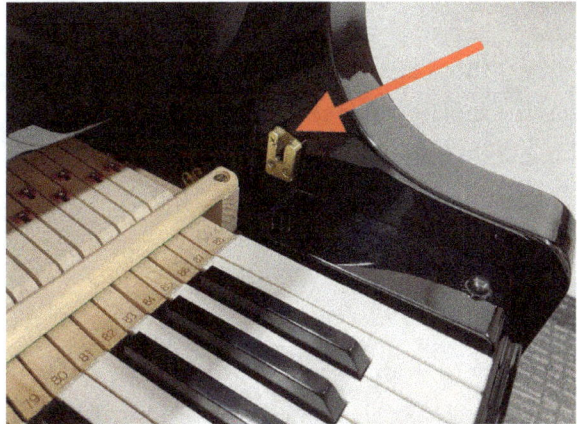

Figure 6.2 – This is the slot into which the fallboard is inserted.

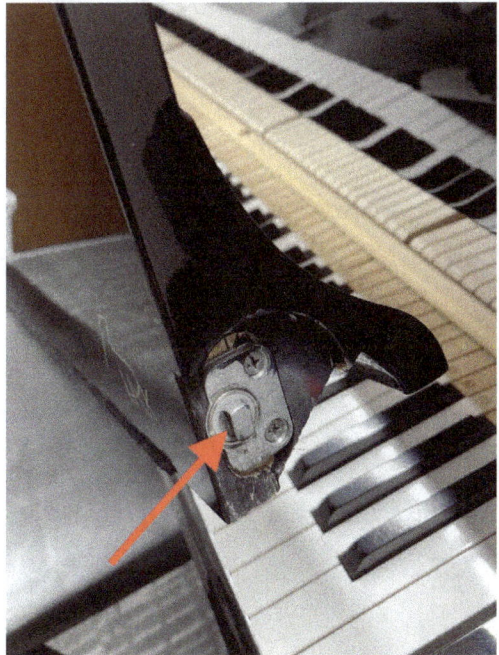

Figure 6.3 – This piece goes into the slots on the sides of the piano.

If that sounded scary, then watch Video 6.1. It's not as bad as it sounds.

Video 6.1 – How to remove a pencil: the easy way.

Method 2: The Less Easy Way

Notice that I didn't say "the hard way". While this method is undoubtedly harder than the first, it is not so hard that you can't figure it out with some coaching. You might be asking how you can know if your piano follows the easy way or the less easy way. To that, I say just try to lift up on the fallboard and if it comes out, then great! If not, then you know that you have a little more work to do.

Your first order of business is to grab a screwdriver. In this method, the fallboard is attached to the two cheekblocks. In order to remove the fallboard, you will need to remove the keyslip, then the fallboard and cheekblocks at the same time. Let's work through this step by step. Mind you, some pianos may follow a slightly different process than the one described here. This procedure is the most common.

Step 1: Remove the keyslip. On some pianos, the keyslip can be pulled straight up to remove it. On others, you will need to remove a few screws from under the piano first.

Step 2: Unscrew the cheekblock screws (the screws are located underneath the sides of the piano).

Step 3: Stand in the middle of the piano. Grab the fallboard firmly with your hands and pull straight up slightly. This should remove both the fallboard and the cheekblocks together.

Step 4: Gently rest the fallboard on the front of the sharp keys.

Step 5: Lift up slightly on one side of the fallboard, then carefully remove the cheekblock from that side and place it back in its spot on the side of the keyboard (Figure 6.4). Rest the fallboard on the front of the sharp keys again.

Figure 6.4 – Removing the cheekblocks.

Step 6: Lift up slightly on the other side of the fallboard and carefully remove that cheekblock. Place it on the side of the keyboard.

Step 7: You can now remove the fallboard and set it somewhere safe.

Step 8: Remove the pencil and other items.

Step 9: To put things back together, start by resting the fallboard on the front of the sharp keys again.

Step 10: Lift up each side of the fallboard and reattach the cheekblocks to the pins on the sides of the fallboard.

Step 11: Stand in the middle of the piano. Grab the fallboard firmly with your hands and lift the fallboard straight up slightly. Don't lift too high as the cheekblocks might fall off.

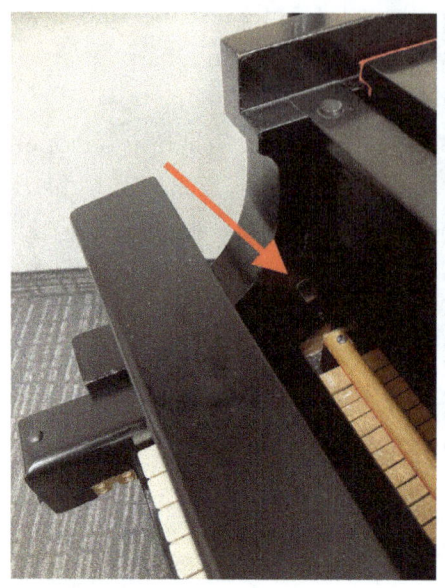

Step 12: Slowly navigate the fallboard and cheekblocks back into the piano. You may need to guide the fallboard up and over a spring on the inside of the piano before it will fall into place (Figure 6.5).

Step 13: Once in place, return the cheekblock screws and the keyslip.

Figure 6.5 (left) – Guide the fallboard over the spring.

Once again, if that sounded scary, then watch Video 6.2. It's almost as bad as it sounds, but not quite.

Video 6.2 – How to remove a pencil: the less easy way.

Question 7

How Do I Open the Lid?

I almost didn't include this question; however, I see piano lids propped open incorrectly far too often to leave it out. I don't even mean in people's homes. I see lids propped open incorrectly in music videos, movies, and even performance venues. To illustrate this, I will provide a series of pictures of what is correct and what is incorrect. Study these images and soon, you too will be watching your favorite TV show and exclaim, "Look at the piano in the background! The lid is propped open incorrectly!"

Before you prop up the lid of a grand piano, you must first open the front section of the piano's lid. The long hinge is not made to bear the weight of this front section. See Figures 7.1 and 7.2.

Figure 7.1 – Incorrect: Front section is open.

Figure 7.2 – Correct: Front section is not open.

If this is a piano you are unfamiliar with, then you should also check the pins that hold the lid to ensure that they haven't fallen out (Figure 7.4). If they have, then the lid will slide right off the piano as you lift up (Figure 7.3)!

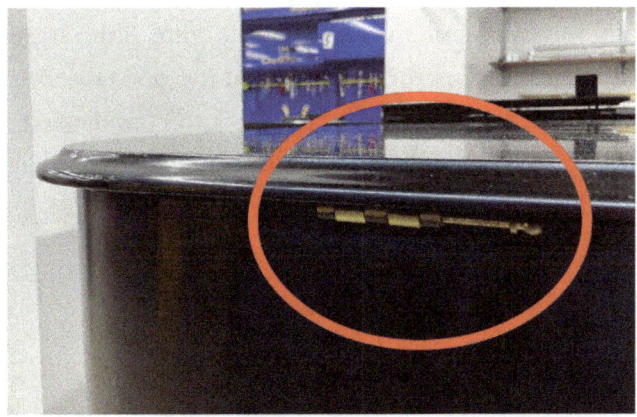

Figure 7.3 – Incorrect: The pin is falling out!

Figure 7.4 – Correct: The pin is secure.

You are now ready to lift the lid. Brace yourself. Piano lids are heavy, especially those on pianos seven feet or longer. You will need to lift the lid high enough that the lid prop doesn't smack the underside of the lid. This could not only damage your piano, but also leave you feeling very silly if people are watching you. So, commit and lift the lid up high.

Now for the hardest part: what hole does the lid prop go into? This is the mistake you will see all over the place (Figure 7.5). The hole closer to the center of the lid is for the full stick; the one closer to the edge of the lid is for the half stick. If that feels too complicated, then just remember that the lid prop must be perpendicular to the lid (Figure 7.6). Think 90-degree angle.

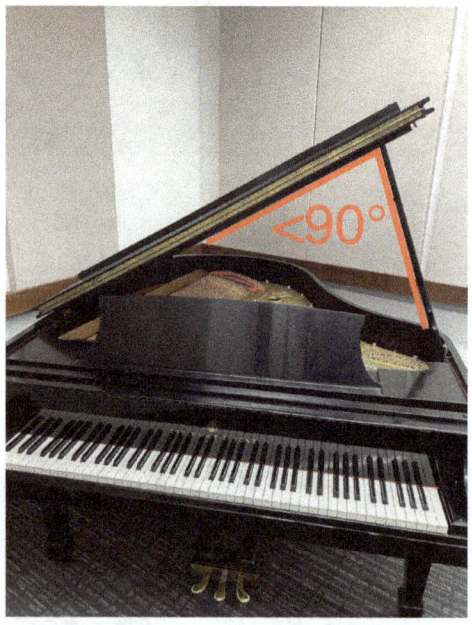

Figure 7.5 – Incorrect: The lid is not at a 90-degree angle.

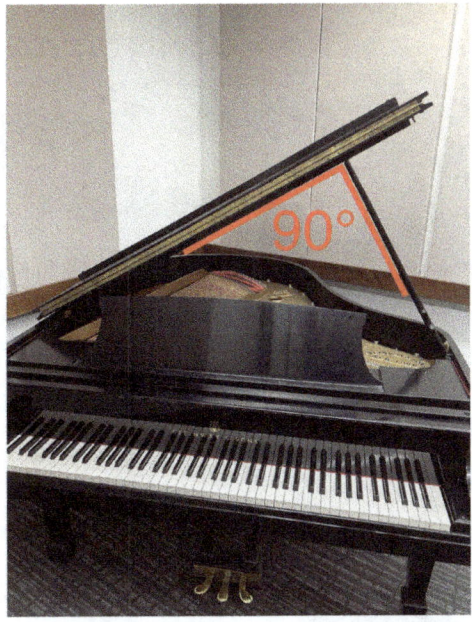

Figure 7.6 – Correct: The lid is at a 90-degree angle.

Some pianos even have a third even shorter lid prop. This option is used primarily for live performances when they only want the lid open wide enough for microphone cables to be run into the piano.

Before we move on, I want to touch briefly on upright piano lids. Most upright pianos have a hinge at the back, which is rarely opened by owners. Many of these lids can be propped open slightly by using a small prop found on the inside of the piano underneath the lid. Open yours to see if you can find the prop.

On some upright pianos, there is a hinge in the middle. These can be opened all the way (Figure 7.7) or propped up by a small prop found on the inside of the piano underneath the lid (Figure 7.8).

Figure 7.7 (Left) – Upright lid with a hinge in the center completely open.

Figure 7.8 (Right) – Upright lid with a hinge in the center propped open.

Some uprights even have a hinge on the bass side (left side), and a lid prop stick attached to the treble side (right side) (Figure 7.9). While these features are nice, in my experience, the temptation to place family photos and other memorabilia on top of an upright piano is far too strong for most people to take advantage of them.

Figure 7.9 – Upright lid prop.

Question 8

Do you Need to Have Perfect Pitch to Tune a Piano?

For some reason, I hear this question all the time. The easiest answer is "No, and thank goodness!" It is estimated that only 0.01% of the population have perfect pitch. There are not nearly enough piano tuners out there as it is. Can you imagine if only 0.01% of the population was even eligible to become one?

For those of you that don't know, perfect pitch (or more accurately, absolute pitch) is the ability possessed by some people to produce a given pitch at will without a reference pitch. So, you could say, "Sing a C" and they could do so without any help. Another way that this gift is manifested is in hearing a tone and properly identifying it. For example, the microwave beeps and they say, "That's an F#!" Obviously, I'm oversimplifying this, but you get the idea.

To tune a piano, you do not need to have perfect pitch, but you do need to have a good ear. Specifically, you need to be able to hear and discern beating in unisons and beat rates in intervals. Are you ready to cover some tuning basics? Ready or not, here we go!

The Note Numbers

The time has come to introduce you to the note numbers on the piano. I don't mean the numbers one through eighty-eight. The system I am referring to is used to quickly identify a note on a piano. I am going to assume that you are already familiar with the note names; A, B, C, D, E, F, G, and their corresponding sharps and flats. Did you know that each C on the piano has a number? The system is fairly simple. The lowest C on the keyboard is C1. The next C is called C2. The next C is called C3. Middle C is C4, and the pattern continues until you reach the C at the very top of the piano, which is called C8. Any note that falls between those Cs gets the same number as the C below it. For example, the E above C2 is E2, and the A above C4 is A4.

"Wait a minute. You said that A4 is the A above middle C (C4), but isn't that technically the fifth A on the keyboard?" Right you are, you hypothetical observer! This is because the notes below C1, are labeled with a zero: A0, A#0 and B0. I hope that doesn't hurt their sense of self-worth.

This system is easier to see than it is to read about. Figure 8.1 should clear things up.

One last thing before we move on. To a piano tuner, every black key is referred to as a sharp. Yes, even A#. I know you probably think of that note as Bb, and so do I when I am thinking about the piano as a musician. When I approach the piano as a tuner however, everything is sharp.

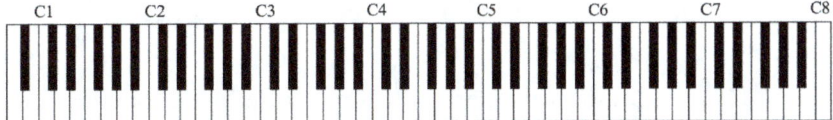

Figure 8.1 – Note numbers on a keyboard.

If you remember nothing else from this book, remember this numbering system. It is *significantly* easier when a pianist tells us that E6 has a particular issue, as opposed to "there is an issue with one of the notes in the area a little bit above middle C, but not quite in the notes on the top of the piano."

What Is Sound?

Imagine you are at a beautiful lake. The clear blue water is perfectly still, reflecting the surrounding scenery. You decide to throw a single stone into the center of the lake. What happens to the water? Hopefully, you know this from experience (if not, then you need to get outside more). The water will make waves that move out peacefully from the location of where your stone entered in the water. These are waves you can see.

Sound is also made of waves, however, these waves we cannot see; and unlike the essentially two-dimensional waves upon the surface of the water, the sound waves your piano creates move outward in a three-dimensional plane, filling every corner of the room with music. Higher tones have faster waves. The human ear can detect waves moving as fast as 20,000 cycles per second. Lower tones have slower waves. The lowest we can hear is around twenty cycles per second. The lowest note on the piano produces a fundamental frequency close to 27.5 cycles per second and the highest note on the piano produces a fundamental frequency around 4,186 cycles per second.

These frequencies, however, are only a part of a bigger picture. This is because when a string vibrates, it doesn't just vibrate at one length. Instead, the string vibrates at multiple different lengths simultaneously. For example, the string will vibrate in its entire length, while also vibrating at half its length, a third of its length, a quarter of its length, and so on (Figure 8.2).

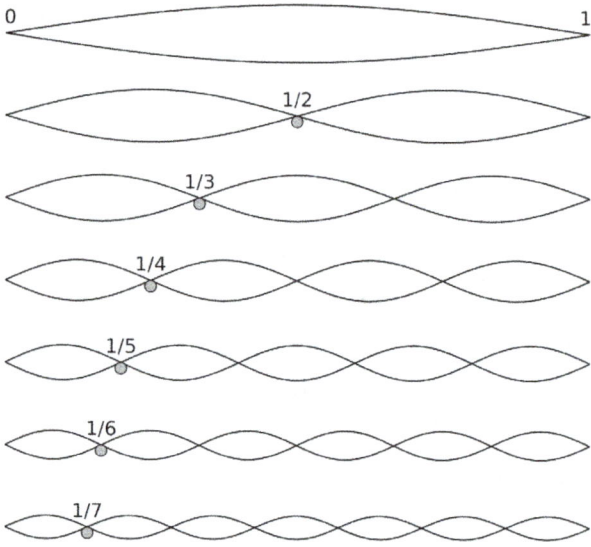

Figure 8.2 – A string vibrating at different lengths.

This creates a series of overtones, or in other words, additional frequencies that are heard at the same time as the fundamental tone of the note. The volume of these overtones is what creates tone color, or timbre.

Have you ever considered how you can hear a flute play middle C and a trumpet play middle C and still tell the two instruments apart? After all, the two instruments are playing the exact same note and those notes have the exact same frequency. Which means that the number of waves produced by the flute and the trumpet are the same. So how can your ear discern between the two?

The answer is the volume of the overtones. While the overtones produced by both a flute and a trumpet are the same, the volume of those overtones are not. In this fascinating  video produced by the YouTube Channel "What Music Really Is", the same note is played over and over on different instruments while the volume of the overtones is depicted visually (Video 8.1).

Video 8.1 – Why different instruments playing the same note sound different.

The Overtone Series

In general, the note being played is called the fundamental. The first overtone above the fundamental is called the first overtone. The second overtone above the fundamental is called the second overtone, and so on. Pretty simple, right? Well, perhaps not surprisingly, the piano is a special case. When referring to the overtone series for the piano, the note being played is not called the fundamental, but instead, the first partial. The first overtone above the note being played is called the second partial, and so on. There is a reason for this deviation from the normal terminology. It happens to be the same reason why you can't use a guitar tuner to tune a piano, but we will get to that shortly.

The overtone series for most musical instruments, including the piano, is shown in the chart below. Don't worry if you aren't super familiar with musical intervals. The main concepts we are striving for can still be understood. Just bear with me as I indulge the more musically trained for a moment.

Overtone (or Partial) Number	The Location
Fundamental (1st Partial)	The note played
1st Overtone (2nd Partial)	An octave above the note played
2nd Overtone (3rd Partial)	An octave & a fifth above the note played
3rd Overtone (4th Partial)	Two octaves above the note played
4th Overtone (5th Partial)	Two octaves & a third above the note played
5th Overtone (6th Partial)	Two octaves & a fifth above the note played

The overtone series keeps going, but piano tuners primarily work with the first six partials, so I'll spare you. Let's look at an example. For A2, the overtone series would look like this:

Overtone (or Partial) Number	The Location	Overtone Series of A2
Fundamental (1st Partial)	The note played	A2
1st Overtone (2nd Partial)	An octave above the note played	A3
2nd Overtone (3rd Partial)	An octave & a fifth above the note played	E4
3rd Overtone (4th Partial)	Two octaves above the note played	A4
4th Overtone (5th Partial)	Two octaves & a third above the note played	C#5
5th Overtone (6th Partial)	Two octaves & a fifth above the note played	E5

Coincident Partials

If you play two notes at the same time, then you have an interval; such as a major third, a fourth, a fifth, a major sixth, an octave, and so on. When two notes are played, two overtone series are produced—one for each note. At a certain point, the two overtone series will have a shared overtone. That overtone is called the coincident partial, because it is at this partial level that the two overtone series coincide.

Let's look at an example. The overtone series of a major third from C3 to E3 would look like this. Notice that the fifth partial of C3 is E5, and the 4th partial of E3 is also E5. This means that E5 (highlighted in green) is the coincident partial.

Overtone (or Partial) Number	The Location	C3	E3
Fundamental (1st Partial)	The Note Played	C3	E3
1st Overtone (2nd Partial)	An Octave Above the Note Played	C4	E4
2nd Overtone (3rd Partial)	An Octave & a Fifth Above the Note Played	G4	B4
3rd Overtone (4th Partial)	Two Octaves Above the Note Played	C5	E5
4th Overtone (5th Partial)	Two Octaves & a Third Above the Note Played	E5	G#5
5th Overtone (6th Partial)	Two Octaves & a Fifth Above the Note Played	G5	B5

Figure 8.3 shows what this example would look like on a keyboard. The red notes are the ones being played. The blue note is the coincident partial.

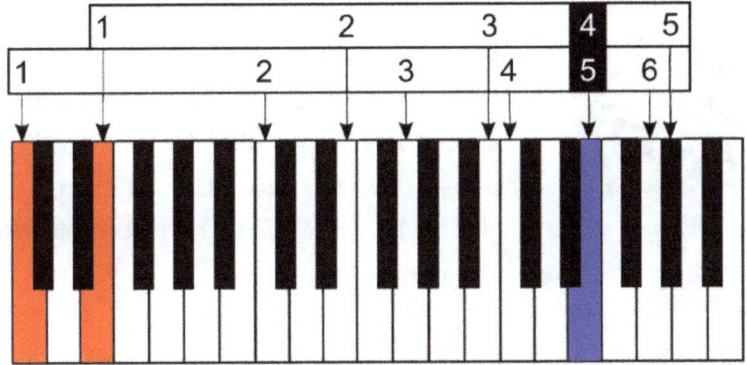

Figure 8.3 – The coincident partial of a major third from C3 to E3 is E5!

How does all of this relate to piano tuning? The answer is that beats occur at coincident partials.

Beating

Beats occur when two sound waves interfere with one another. If the two sound waves move up and down in sync with each other, then they are in phase and there is no beating. If the two sound waves move out of sync with one another, then they are out of phase and will produce a phenomenon that piano tuners call beating.

In Video 8.2, a sine wave that cycles 440 times per second is played. This is the most common frequency for A4 in the piano. A second sine wave will then be played that cycles 444 times per second. These sine waves do not contain any overtones. The two sine waves will then be played together. This will result in a beat rate of four beats per second (444 minus 440).

Video 8.2 – A440 & A444.

Could you hear the beating? Let's slow it down. In Video 8.3, the sine wave that cycles 440 times per second will be played with a sine wave that cycles 441 times per second, resulting in a beat rate of one beat per second. This beat rate will then be decreased to a half a beat per second, and then decreased again.

Video 8.3 – A440 & A441.

Could you hear the beating as it slowed down? This is what piano tuners are listening to while they tune. For example, when tuning the strings of a unison (aka the two or three strings for the same note), the tuner will strive to remove all of the beating.

Here is a video of a unison with one of the strings out of sync with the other two (Video 8.4). Can you hear the beating? Then, as the unison is tuned, can you hear the beating decrease and eventually stop?

Video 8.4 – Beating in a unison.

So, is that all there is to it? If all of the unisons are in tune, then does that mean the piano is in tune as well? If only it was that easy. In Video 8.5, I will play C3 and C4. Notice how both unisons are in tune. I will then play both notes at the same time. The octave from C3 to C4 is full of beats! Where are those beats coming from? They aren't coming from the unisons.

Video 8.5 – Beating in an octave.

The answer is that not only do the unisons need to be in tune, but also the distance between the notes needs to be correct *for the piano to be in tune*. Your first thought might be to tune every interval without beats, like we did with the unisons. Again, it's not that easy. When tuning intervals on a keyboard instrument, there will always be beats. The question is, which intervals will contain them? Over the centuries, different approaches have been used, from Pythagorean, to Meantone, and a collection of Well Temperament tunings. Each of these systems had their own strengths and weaknesses. Today, the musical community seems to have settled on Equal Temperament as the acceptable one-size-fits-all option. In light of this, it might surprise you to hear that in Equal Temperament not a single interval is tuned without beats. When tuning thirds, fourths, fifths, sixths, and octaves, the tuner must intentionally leave the appropriate amount of beats in each interval to produce the result that we have collectively come to regard as "in tune."

Fun Fact: This is why choirs and string instruments take on a different character when singing acapella or playing in a string quartet. Whenever a piano is involved, the musicians must match the tuning of the piano. Remove the piano, and the singers and instrumentalists are free to listen and tune to each other. When they do this, they often reduce the amount of beating in the intervals; sometimes without realizing they are doing it. Barbershop quartets take it a step further and intentionally sing in Just Intonation to achieve their unique sound, which is impossible to do with a piano.

Now that you know what to listen for, let's return to the point we arrived at earlier; namely, that beats occur at coincident partials. Each overtone has a sound wave. But as long as that sound wave has room to cycle freely, it will not create a beat. Remember, beats occur when two sound waves interfere with each other. So, returning to our C3-E3 major third example (see Figure 8.3). Each sound wave has its own space to cycle freely except for E5, the coincident partial. When C3 and E3 are played together, the two sound waves at E5 start to interfere with each other. This means that the beating for that interval can be heard at that coincident partial.

Let's listen to an example so you can hear what I mean. Video 8.6 is an excerpt from Rick Baldassin's *On Pitch Companionship DVD Volume I: Octave Types & Tests*. In it, the major third from C3 to E3 is played. At first listen, this might just sound like a normal major third played on a piano. Then, an audio filter will be placed over the coincident partial E5 to highlight the beating. The C3-E3 major third is then played again. Can you hear the beating the second time? If not, then watch the video again. Could you hear the beating on the third or fourth time? If you can, then your ears have what it takes to tune a piano.

Video 8.6 – Beating in a major third from *On Pitch Companionship DVD Volume I.*

Try this at home. Go to your piano and press down the keys for C3 and E3 slowly so the hammers don't strike the strings. Keep holding those notes down so that the dampers for C3 and E3 are raised. Then strike E5 quickly and release it. The damper for E5 has now stopped the vibration of E5's strings. Meaning that any sound you hear is a result of the C3 and E3 strings vibrating sympathetically. Can you hear the beating?

Now try striking the other notes in the overtone series of C3 and E3. For example, while holding down C3 and E3, strike E4, G4, G5 and B5. These notes will also cause the strings of C3 and E3 to vibrate sympathetically, but they will not result in a beat. Only playing the coincident partial E5 will create a beat.

While you should still try this at home, Video 8.7 is a video of me performing the exercise described above. Of course, all intervals have  at least one coincident partial, and thus at least one beat rate. This means that this same process can be performed with any interval by holding down the notes of the interval and striking the coincident partial(s) to sympathetically excite the beat rates.

Video 8.7 – Ghosting a major third.

Why a Guitar Tuner Won't Work

It's not common, but more than once I have received a phone call, usually from the wife of the family, to come out and fix a piano that their husband tried to tune with a socket wrench and a guitar tuner. Now, there are a lot of things wrong with this approach, but let's focus on the issue of using a guitar tuner. Most guitar tuning apps are free, or only a couple of dollars; however, at this writing, piano tuning apps hold the number one and number two slots for the most expensive apps on the App Store – at $999.99 and $599.99 respectively. Most other piano tuning apps are in the $300 range, which easily puts them in the top 10. What is it about the piano that makes their tuning devices so much more expensive?

The answer is a concept known as inharmonicity. Most string instruments vibrate harmonically. This means that when a cello bows the note A2, the overtones of that note follow a perfect mathematical progression. The frequency of the fundamental A2 is 110 cycles per second, its first overtone A3 will cycle exactly 220 times per second. Its third overtone A4 will cycle 440 times per second, and A5 will cycle 880 times per second, and so on.

When the hammer strikes the strings of the piano, those strings do not vibrate harmonically, they vibrate inharmonically. This means that the overtones do not follow a mathematical progression that uses whole numbers. The frequency of the first partial A2 will still cycle 110 times per second. However, the second partial A3 will not cycle 220 times per second, but slightly above this whole number multiple, for example 220.5 times per second. The fourth partial A4 might cycle 441 times per second, and A5 might cycle around 884 times per second. Notice that the deviation increases with each overtone.

To make matters worse, each piano has a different amount of inharmonicity. Upright pianos and smaller grand pianos have more inharmonicity, while larger grand pianos have less. Since the amount of deviation changes from one piano to the next, this means that the tuning for each piano is unique, and the compromises needed to achieve the ideal beat rates for each interval will change. As you might imagine, this makes the math tremendously difficult—hundreds of dollars more difficult, apparently.

The effects of inharmonicity are particularly felt when tuning intervals with multiple coincident partials. The major third from C3 to E3 had one coincident partial, which means it only had one beat rate. But what about an octave from C3 to C4? The overtone series for the two notes of an octave are extremely similar as shown in Figure 8.4. In the image, the notes being played (C3 and C4) are indicated by an "x" on each note. The blue notes show the coincident partial levels.

Octave

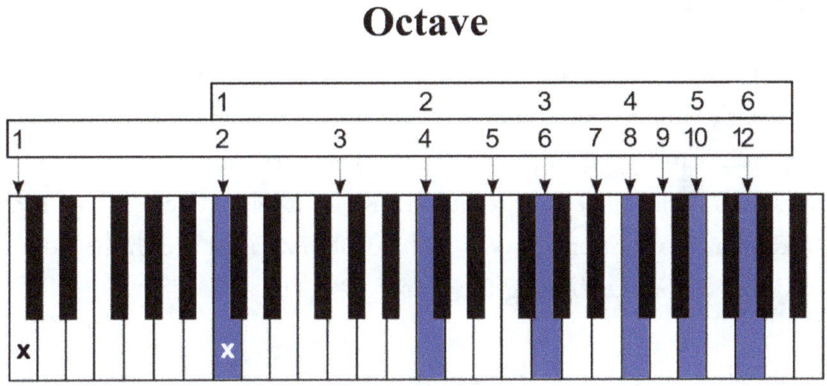

Figure 8.4 – Octaves have many sets of coincident partials, each with its own beat rate.

Look at all those coincident partials! Remember, beats occur at coincident partials. This means that octaves have multiple beat rates. Octaves are kind of a big deal in music, and so they need to sound nice, but because of inharmonicity it is impossible to tune all of these coincident partial levels without beats. The tuner must choose the best option and leave beats in the rest.

Let's watch another video taken from Rick Baldassin's *On Pitch Companionship DVD Volume I: Octave Types & Tests*. In Video 8.8, the same octave is played multiple times. Each time a filter is placed over a different partial level. Only the 8:4 level has no beats (which is C6, the eighth partial of the C3 and the fourth partial of C4). All of the other coincident partial levels have beats.

Video 8.8 – Inharmonicity from *On Pitch Companionship DVD Volume I.*

At this point, you may be asking: "If there is beating in every partial level but one, how do you know which one to pick? Which compromise will result in the best sounding octave?" If, in fact, you are asking this extremely bookish question, then know that you have gone full piano-nerd and I can't cure you of that. The answer to those questions could fill an entire book. In fact, it has. My colleague, Rick Baldassin, has written a book entitled *On Pitch*. I'd recommend you read that if you are longing for more.

That said, I imagine that most of you are thinking, "When is this going to end? I've had my fill of tuning theory, thank you very much." This is a good perspective to have gained from all of this. I remember the allure of making money by learning how to tune pianos. "How hard could it be?" I told myself. Turns out, it takes more than a socket wrench and a guitar tuner. To slander the immortal words of JFK, we do these things not because they are easy, but because we thought they would be.

Section 2

How do I Care for My Piano?

Question 9

How do I Clean My Piano?

"Sorry about the dust!"

Now, that's a phrase I hear all the time. The funny part is, more often than not, the dust doesn't bother me nearly as much as the poor shape of the tuning, or the other issues the piano may have. Cleaning a piano isn't actually as bad as people think. You just need a little bit of guidance to do it safely.

The Case

I'll confess, as a piano technician, I am much better acquainted with the upkeep of the inside of the piano than I am with the outside. So, to avoid venturing too far into unfamiliar territory, suffice it to say that pianos typically come in one of two types of finishes. First are lacquer finishes (see the piano on the right in Figure 9.1). These aren't as shiny or reflective. The finish looks more like what you would expect to see in other pieces of wood furniture. A classic black piano with this finish would be referred to as "ebony satin". These pianos can be dusted using a microfiber cloth.

The second common type is polyester finishes (see the piano on the left in Figure 9.1). These are much shinier and reflective. A classic black piano with this finish would be referred to as "polished ebony". These pianos tend to show fingerprints and smudges more noticeably, especially if the light hits them just right. There are a number of outstanding commercial cleaners and polishes sold for all piano finishes. For me personally, I've found that a little bit of Windex on a microfiber cloth works great on polyester finishes.

For more detailed cleaning instructions, or if the finish of your piano needs to be repaired, please consult your piano technician—they may be a qualified refinisher. If not, then they should be able to refer one to you.

Figure 9.1 (Left) – The two most common types of piano finishes. Lacquer finish on the right, polyester finish on the left.

The Keys

Let's face it, our hands are gross. People eat, use the restroom, and do all sorts of things before they sit down to play the piano. Don't think about it too hard … maybe it's too late. I'd bet you are already feeling the urge to stop reading and go clean your keys right now. When was the last time you cleaned the keys of your piano? Don't think about that too hard either…

Since most keys are made from plastic now, they are fairly easy to clean. Once again, there are commercial products available, but I typically find myself using a little Windex on a microfiber cloth. Of course, not all keytops are made of plastic. Your piano may have keytops made from ivory and if so, then they are likely yellowed and chipped. Nearly everyone who owns a piano with ivory keytops seems to dream about replacing them, and they ask me for my advice. So here is my advice. Warning: it might not be what you want to hear.

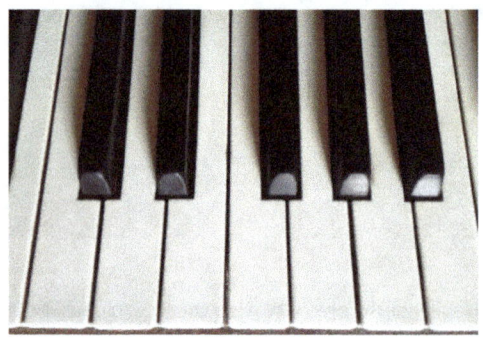

Figure 9.2 (Top) – Keys before cleaning.

Figure 9.3 (Bottom) – Keys after cleaning.

Most piano manufacturers stopped using ivory during the 1950s, meaning that the *newest* a piano can be with ivory keys is over 70 years old. We will talk more about this in Section 3, but the average musical lifespan of a piano is around 50 years. Of course, most families hold on to their piano for decades beyond the 50-year mark, but after that point, while sentimental value may be high, the musical and financial value of the instrument is very low. The cost to replace the keytops almost always exceeds the value of the instrument. Additionally, only replacing the keytops completely ignores the condition of the action parts and structural components (such as the soundboard or pinblock). So the family might spend a sum of money to end up with a lovely looking keyboard on a piano that can barely be played or tuned. In nearly all cases, that money would have been much better spent if invested into a newer instrument. More on this later—back to cleaning!

Underneath the Strings and Around the Tuning Pins

These are two of the most difficult places to clean. How many of you have tried to use your vacuum to suck up the dust on the soundboard? It doesn't work, right? No vacuum is strong enough. The secret is actually to blow the dust from off the soundboard. A can of compressed air works wonders to clear the dust from under the strings and around the tuning pins. Of course, if you have a portable air compressor in your garage, then that will work too. Yes, this does get dust all over your living room, but at least you can clean it up once it's out from under the strings.

If it's been a couple of decades since the soundboard was cleaned, then even compressed air might not be enough. You will need to have your technician come out and do a deep cleaning. They should have specialized tools for this.

Video 9.1 – Cleaning a piano with compressed air.

The Plate and The Dampers

The final two areas we will discuss are the plate and the dampers. The plate is one of the easiest to clean. Feel free to lift the lid and use a microfiber cloth to dust off any metal surface in the belly of the piano with no fear of harming the instrument.

The dampers are a little trickier. Each damper head is attached to a wire. If you aren't careful, you can accidentally bend those wires and cause the dampers to no longer function optimally. The secret is to dust them off parallel to the strings as shown in Video 9.2. If that makes you nervous, then just have your technician do it when they come to service the piano.

Video 9.2 – Cleaning dampers.

Question 10

How Do I Move My Piano?

Hire professional piano movers. Next question.

Okay fine, I'll offer a little bit more, but not much.

Moving a piano isn't easy. They are incredibly heavy, and they are also at the most risk of being damaged when they are moved. Hiring professionals is the easiest way to ensure that your instrument is protected.

An upright piano is a little easier to move. The process usually involves two or more people lifting the piano straight onto a moving dolly. With the pedals centered on the dolly, an upright piano is fairly balanced. Moving blankets can be placed around the piano to strap it to the dolly without harming the finish. The piano can then be rolled onto a moving truck where it can be secured.

Figure 10.1 – Upright piano strapped to a dolly. Photo courtesy of Adeline Bouwhuis.

Not surprisingly, grand pianos present their own set of challenges. For one, the piano can't fit through a doorway while on its legs. The moving process typically involves supporting the pedal lyre, removing the front leg on the bass side of the piano, and then tipping the piano onto a board on a dolly. This board is called a skid board. With the piano on its side, the pedal lyre and remaining two legs can be removed. The piano is then secured to the skid board and moved through any doorways and onto a moving truck (Video 10.1).

Video 10.1 – Time-lapse of moving a grand piano.

This process is reversed when tipping the piano back down onto its legs. Before the movers leave, play a note to make sure the piano isn't

ringing. Remember way back in Question 5 when we learned about the damper tray and how it is pushed up by the pedal system to raise all of the dampers? The pitman that connects the pedal system to the damper tray can become dislodged during the moving process (Figure 10.2). Do not let the movers leave without fixing this issue! Yet another reason to hire professional piano movers.

Figure 10.2 (Above) – Dislodged pitman. This is causing the dampers to be lifted off the strings and the piano to ring (as if the sustain pedal was being pressed).

Of course, moving a piano up or down stairs complicates this process even further. So much so that it is not uncommon for piano movers to charge by the stair (Figure 10.3).

Figure 10.3 (Left) – Moving an upright piano up a flight of stairs.

Finally, as I am sure you have been told all your life, the piano needs to be tuned after it is moved. We will talk about why that is in Question 12.

Question 11

What Should I Look for in a Piano Technician?

For many people, their piano is a part of their family. I believe that it is for this reason that finding a piano technician can feel more like finding a hairdresser than a plumber. The emotional connection to the instrument is powerful and compels the owner to seek out a similar connection with a technician. The question is, how do you know who to trust?

Piano tuning is an unregulated industry. If you wanted to be a piano tuner, you could print off some business cards, build a website, and off you go, even with no experience. So, what should you look for in a technician?

First, in the United States, there is really only one professional certification available. This is becoming a Registered Piano Technician (RPT) through the Piano Technicians Guild. In order to obtain this certification, a technician must pass a series of exams that test their competency in tuning, regulation and repair. This is the best place to start. Visit www.ptg.org to find an RPT in your area.

That said, there are many great technicians out there who are not members of the Piano Technicians Guild, and of course, there is also no guarantee that just because someone is a Registered Piano Technician that they will be the best fit for you and your piano. Another thing to look for would be formal education of any kind, in particular, if they attended the North Bennet Street School in Boston, or if they have received any manufacturer training. Online reviews and old-fashioned word-of-mouth also go a long way in this industry.

Be wary of anyone who leans *exclusively* on their years of experience. There is a big difference between someone who has twenty-five years of experience, and someone who has experienced the same year twenty-five times. I'd happily take a Registered Piano Technician with some manufacturer training and only ten years of experience, over someone who's been tuning as a side hustle on-and-off for the last three decades.

Depending on where you live, your options may be limited, but a good rule of thumb is this: look for a technician who is on the more expensive side for your area and is booked out for a couple of weeks. If you find someone who meets those parameters, then there's a high chance that technician does excellent work.

Question 12

How Often Should I Tune My Piano?

A few summers ago, I was asked to tune for an outdoor concert. The piano was under a canopy, but when I arrived to tune for the rehearsal, the sun was perfectly positioned to shine directly onto the piano's strings. I asked the stage manager to reposition the canopy so that the piano could be in the shade and hoped for the best.

An hour or so later, I was feeling pretty good about how the piano turned out and left to grab some dinner before returning to tune the piano again for the performance. To my dismay, a summer storm began to roll in as I left the venue. I could see the wall of dark clouds heading straight toward me as I felt the humidity in the air increasing.

When I returned a few hours later, the outdoor venue was caught in an incredible downpour of hot summer rain. I stood in the covered recording booth with the audio engineer, staring awkwardly at the stage with the piano on it, knowing that at some point I would need to trek the length of the venue in the rain to tune the piano again.

While I waited for the deluge to let up a little, the audio engineer told me about the rehearsal, "I've never heard anything like it," he said, "You could literally hear the piano going more and more out of tune as the clouds rolled in and it began to rain!"

Bracing myself, I soon made my way back to the piano. The tuning was in worse shape than it was when I had arrived earlier that day to find it baking in the sun. It seemed as though it had been years since the piano had been tuned, when in reality, it had only been a couple of hours.

By this point, the concert was supposed to have started, but it had been postponed in hopes that the rain would eventually subside. I figured it couldn't get any more humid than it already was, and so I started to tune. Halfway through, a section of the canopy collapsed from the puddle that it had collected, spilling buckets of water mere feet away from the piano. Exhausted, I finished the tuning as best I could under the circumstances and decided there was nothing else I could do. Eventually the concert did start, just in time for the sun to set and the temperature to change mid-performance. Yikes!

So, what causes a piano to go out of tune?

Reason #1: Change in Relative Humidity

The first and most impactful reason is changes to the piano's environment, specifically temperature and relative humidity. As we have learned, the piano is made of organic materials. As the moisture content of the wood increases or decreases with the relative humidity of the room, the soundboard, bridges, and pinblock all expand or contract, moving the strings along with them. Which is why the poor piano left outside in the baking sun and torrential rain didn't stand a chance.

Let's consider the implications of this in your home. While you likely won't experience such a dramatic shift in climate as I did that fateful afternoon, your piano will slowly transition from one environment to another as the seasons change. This is why nearly all piano manufacturers recommend a tuning every six months. This frequency accounts for the changes in the seasons. From the dry, cold winters, to the hot, humid summers. Depending on where you live, the amount of change the seasons bring will vary. When I worked in the Northeast, many of my clients tuned their piano twice a year. When I lived in Florida, many people opted for a tuning once a year, since the difference in the relative humidity between the seasons was much smaller. On a new piano, four tunings within the first year is what is recommended.

I sometimes hear people say that they don't need to tune their piano because it hasn't been played much since it was last tuned. The reality is, even if you aren't playing your piano, the seasons are.

This is also why you should tune a piano each time it is moved. It isn't the act of moving the piano that causes it to go out of tune. It is the changing of its environment. This means that if you move your piano from one side of the room to the other, it likely will hold its tuning just fine. If you tip the piano onto its side, roll it outdoors and onto a moving truck, and drive it to your new place across town (or especially across the country), then your piano will definitely need a tuning. For the best results, give the piano a week or so to acclimate to its new environment before having it tuned.

When positioning your piano in your home, avoid placing it over a vent, near your front door or fireplace, or anywhere the strings or soundboard will be in direct sunlight during certain hours of the day. There are a handful of products available to help minimize the effects of these changes in a piano's environment. Not surprisingly, I found that these products were more common in the Northeast than in the South. It is important to note that these climate control systems typically require that the piano owner perform some routine maintenance tasks in order for them to function properly. It is nothing terribly difficult, but if you are the kind of person who forgets to water your houseplants, then these systems might not be the best option for you. Ultimately, while these products may help reduce the more dramatic effects of a changing environment, they do not remove the need for an annual or bi-annual tuning.

Reason #2: Playing the Piano

Of course, playing your piano can also cause it to go out of tune, but the effect of this variable is not nearly as dramatic as people think. In fact, if the technician tunes with a concert level of stability (something which takes years to master), then the pianist should be able to play as hard as musically required without any of the strings slipping. However, that stability only lasts as long as the environment stays exactly the same as when the piano was tuned. Another story may help to illustrate this point.

This time, I was asked to tune for a multi-day piano festival. Fortunately, this concert venue was indoors! I arrived in the late afternoon, a few hours before the concert. The piano had been delivered the night before to give it some time to acclimate to its new environment. Before I arrived, the pianists from the festival had been allowed to spend time practicing on the piano. Not surprisingly, by the time I showed up, the piano was far from ready for its concert debut. Fortunately, the piano was in excellent condition and I was able to tune it with a high level of stability. I took my seat and the concert started. After an hour or so of showcasing the incredible talent of these pianists, I returned to the piano to touch it up during intermission. As expected, there wasn't much for me to do. The piano had remained remarkably stable during the first half of the concert.

When the concert ended, the audience left, the lights were turned off, and the piano was left on stage overnight. While the piano didn't move, its environment did change from a hall full of people and the stage lights on, to the dark stage overnight. The next morning, the festival participants attended masterclasses and practiced on that same piano. When I arrived the next evening, there were small things to touch up on the piano. Which is interesting, because the tuning was the same. During the concert, it was solid, but during the practice hours of the morning, it started to show hints of weakness. I believe this is due to the changes that occurred in the piano's environment from one day to the next. The wood shifted slightly, which destabilized the tuning slightly. This is why most concert pianos are tuned before each performance.

So, perhaps Reason #1 and Reason #2 are more connected than people realize. Significant changes to the relative humidity of the piano's environment will cause the piano to go out of tune regardless of whether or not it is played. This typically manifests itself as an entire section of notes going sharp or flat depending on the season. Playing, especially hard playing, can reveal any weaknesses in the stability caused by smaller environmental shifts. This is typically manifested by a single string of a unison slipping.

Of course, if the tuner doesn't leave the tuning pin in a stable location, then the string will slip during hard playing, even without a change to the piano's environment. In these cases, the weakness was left there by the tuner, not introduced by a shifting environment. To be fair, on an instrument with an older or lower quality pinblock, the tuner might not be able to provide the highest level of stability. All the same, this is yet another reason to select a qualified technician to service your instrument.

Pitch Raises

Piano manufacturers recommend a tuning every six months. Depending on the climate where you live, you may find that a yearly tuning meets your needs. But what happens if a piano goes a long time without a tuning?

After a number of years, the pitch of the piano will fall so dramatically that it can no longer be tuned in a single pass. Think of it like throwing a basketball into a hoop. I know, I know. A sports analogy in a book about pianos. Just bear with me.

In basketball, making a layup is easy. The player is right by the hoop. Making it from the free throw line is a little trickier. The player is now fifteen feet away from the hoop, but even still, most NBA players make a free throw 80% of the time. What about a three pointer? The player is now at least twenty-two feet away from the hoop. Suddenly, the percentage drops to around 40%. Now, can you imagine the likelihood of making a half-court shot? It's somewhere around 1%.

Piano tuners measure how flat or sharp a piano is in cents, with one hundred cents in each half step. Over the course of a year or so, a piano tends to fall around one to fifteen cents flat. Within this range, the piano strings can be pulled up to pitch without much issue. Once a piano is over fifteen to twenty cents flat, then the piano will likely need to be tuned twice. The first tuning is called a pitch raise. The goal of this first pass is to simply raise the pitch of the piano to be closer to the target. Only then can the tuner hope to tune the piano and actually make the shot.

If it has been over five years since a piano has been tuned, or perhaps even over ten or twenty (naturally, I'm not talking about *your* piano here, right?), then the piano might be over fifty cents flat. Tuning this piano in one pass is like making a half-court shot, which is nearly impossible. The best course of action is to move closer to the target. A pitch raise pass is used to get the strings of the piano within a few cents of the target pitch. Once within this range, the tuner can finally tune the piano with the accuracy and stability your piano deserves.

Many tuners will charge extra for a pitch raise pass, but don't let this be the primary reason to avoid needing one. Your piano was designed to be played at a certain pitch. It will sound better and your music making will be more enjoyable if you tune your piano regularly; which in a home, means at least yearly or bi-yearly. Additionally, the tuning isn't the only thing that will fall into disrepair if your piano is neglected. More on that in the next question.

Question 13

Is Tuning All My Piano Needs?

Think of your piano like a car. I know, first a sports analogy, and now this! At least I know that even if you aren't a sports fan, you likely have some experience maintaining a car. Tunings are like oil changes. They are absolutely critical to the health of your car and are needed around once or twice a year, depending on how much you drive. While you may not know exactly how your car works, you do know that oil changes are not all that your car will need over the course of its life. Brakes pads will need changing, wheels will need aligning, transmissions may need replacing, new tires will be needed, and so on.

Similarly, your piano cannot live on tunings alone. Allow me to introduce you to the Three T's of Piano Maintenance.

These are:

1. Tune
2. Touch
3. Tone

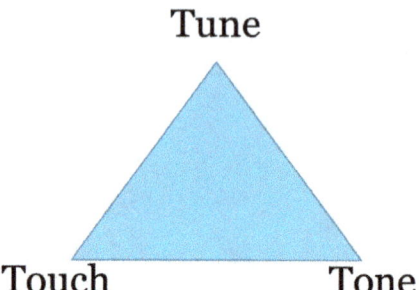

We covered tuning in the last question. Let's now consider touch and tone.

Touch (Regulation)

How does it feel to play your piano? Does it feel like driving a truck or a sports car? Does your piano repeat consistently? Can you play at incredibly soft dynamic levels and feel a sense of control? Or perhaps most revealing, do your kids tell you that their music is easier to play on their teacher's piano than on your own?

A piano can be perfectly in tune and still be riddled with problems with the touch. Remember the four main components of the piano action from Question 3? They were the key, the hammer, the damper, and the wippen. Within each of these components are adjustment points that can improve the touch of your piano. These include: adjustments to the height of the key, how far the key travels, how far the hammer is from the string at rest, before escapement, and when caught by the backcheck, the position of the jack, the moment the damper is lifted, and the tension of the spring in the wippen of a grand piano—the list goes on and on. Adjusting these points is referred to as regulation (Figure 13.2).

Figure 13.2 – Some of the regulation points in the grand piano action.

If you own a grand piano, then you can quickly see if your piano would benefit from regulation services by trying the follow two keystrokes:

1. **The Control Test** (Video 13.1)
   Play a key very slowly. The hammer should:
   - ☐ Rise until it almost touches the strings
   - ☐ Fall back down slightly
   - ☐ Rise slightly toward the strings again
2. **The Repetition Test** (Video 13.2)
   Play a key normally and hold it down. The hammer should:
   - ☐ Be caught around a finger's distance from the strings
   Slowly let up on the key. The hammer should:
   - ☐ Rise quickly toward the strings

How many of the five checkboxes above does your piano satisfy? While they certainly aren't the only indicators, these constitute a good baseline. If your piano isn't checking all five, then you know that the action is performing well below its potential. Even if you don't understand what any of it means.

Remember too that consistency is critical for your piano to perform well. Use these tests on notes in the bass, midrange, and treble to ensure that your entire piano action is functioning properly.

Video 13.1 (Left) – The Control Test, correct and incorrect

Video 13.2 (Right) – The Repetition Test, correct and incorrect

Other factors that influence the touch of the piano include the friction in the key and in the action parts. Each key has two slots (called mortises) with a piece of cloth in each (indicated by the red arrows in Figures 13.3 and 13.4). These cloth bushings can get tight with time and need to be eased. They can also become loose and require that new bushings be inserted. This replacement process is called rebushing.

Test if your key bushings are loose by moving the fronts of your keys side-to-side. There should be a small amount of side play, but not so much that the keys visibly misalign themselves or click against the key pins like they do in Video 13.3.

Video 13.3 – Loose key bushings.

Figure 13.3 (Left) – Cloth bushing under the front of the key.

Figure 13.4 (Right) – Cloth bushing at the rotation point in the middle of the key.

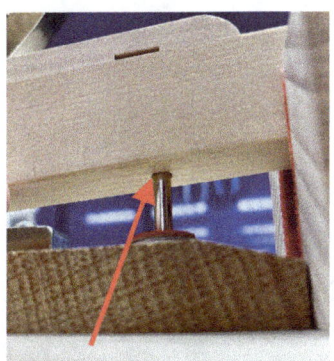

The arrow in Figure 13.5 points to the balance rail hole. While not a cloth bushing, this balance rail hole can also be eased to reduce the amount of friction in your piano's action.

Figure 13.5 – Balance rail hole under the middle of the key.

Friction is also found at the points of rotation in the wippen, hammer, and damper. In each, there is a small pin inserted into a cloth bushing (circled in red in Figure 13.6). These pins can become tight or loose with time. The process of removing the old pins and inserting new ones in order to address friction is called repinning.

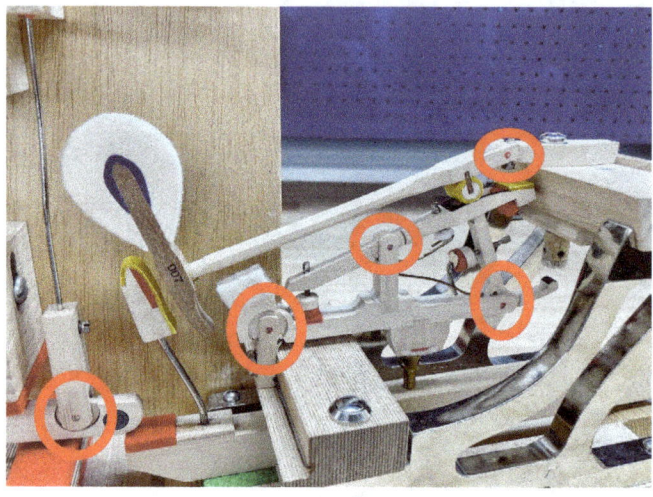

Figure 13.6 – Pins at each point of rotation in the grand piano action.

If you've ever had a sticky key on your piano, then there is a good chance the cause was either a tight key bushing or a tight center pin.

Most technicians will offer regulation services ranging from a few hours to a few days. These services can be performed in your home, or the action of your piano may be removed and taken to a shop. Talk to your technician to determine what your piano needs. Most pianos should be regulated every five to ten years. Rebushing and repinning services will take multiple days of work and will generally be performed outside of your home. These services should be considered at least once in an in-home piano's life, especially if it is a grand.

Tone (Voicing)

How does your piano sound? Is it too bright? Too mellow? Do the top octaves sound offensively shrill? Is the midrange so loud that it overpowers the melody octaves in the treble? These things can all be adjusted.

Stop reading and tap your table or desk with your finger. Now tap it with your knuckle. Hear the difference? These two taps sound different because the tip of your finger is softer than the bone of your knuckle. Think of the difference in tone created by striking the same note of xylophone with an acrylic mallet and a yarn mallet. Thanks to our incredible wooly friends, the sheep, the tension in the felts of the piano hammers can also be adjusted to change the tone of your piano. This process is called voicing.

While there are a number of different voicing techniques, the most common is to adjust the hammer felts using needles attached to specialized tools (Figure 13.7). Needling different regions of the hammer will produce different effects.

Figure 13.7 (Left) – Needling the top of the hammer.

One of the most common voicing issues is when a note will "stick out" or sound accented when compared to its neighbors. In Video 13.4, I am playing up and down the keyboard with the same amount

of force on each note. Can you hear the note that sounds accented? After the problematic note is voiced, can you hear other notes that stick out? This is just one example of how voicing techniques are used.

Video 13.4 – Voicing for evenness.

Other factors that influence the tone of your piano include the depth of the hammer string grooves and how effectively the hammers strike the strings. The string grooves can be removed by sanding the felt of the hammer. This process is called hammer filing.

The effectiveness of the hammers striking the strings can be increased by aligning the hammers to the strings, ensuring that the hammers travel up and down in a straight line and that the three strings of each unison are struck at the exact same time. Let's imagine that the top of the hammer is slightly sloped so that it hits the left and middle strings before striking the right string (the second option from the left in Figure 13.8). If this were the case, then the left and middle sections of the top of the hammer could be sanded down slightly until all three strings were stuck at the exact same moment. This process is called mating the hammer to the string.

The slow-motion footage featured in Video 13.5 was created by Scott Murphy, one of the piano technicians at the Juilliard School. He received a research grant from the Piano Technicians Guild Foundation to create them. They clearly illustrate how critical it is for the hammers to be mated to the strings in order to improve the overall tone of the piano.

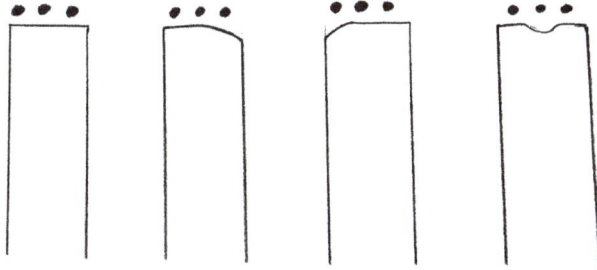

Figure 13.8 – The many ways the slope of the hammer can affect how effectively it strikes the strings.

Video 13.5 – Slow-motion video of a mated and unmated hammer striking the strings of a piano.

Voicing services are provided in the home and can last from an hour to many hours depending on the scope of the work. Be prepared to work together with your technician as you seek the ideal tone for your piano. Typically, tuning and regulation are performed before serious voicing begins.

At times, I hear people complain about their piano. They loved the piano when they bought it, but now they are sure that they need to replace it. The first thing I ask them is when the piano was last regulated and voiced. Usually, they reply that while they've had it tuned year after year, they have never thought to invest in regulation or voicing services. I promise them that if they do, then they will rediscover the love they once had for the instrument for a fraction of the cost of replacing it. The qualities they loved have simply slipped away due to neglect of the piano's touch and tone.

Question 14

How Can I Help My Technician?

This book was supposed to cover the most frequently asked questions I receive as a piano technician. I confess, this question is not so frequently asked, but I wish it was! Honestly, just by deciding to read this book, you have begun a process of educating yourself about your instrument that will help you and your technician develop a better relationship. Your piano technician is one of your greatest allies in your musical pursuits. They are also a person with a life, aspirations, interests, and hobbies of their own—it is important to remember that. In my experience, there are two types of piano owners: those who know your name, respect your time and thank you for your work, and those who treat you like a nameless janitor. Both types pay for my services, but I'll let you guess which one I enjoy working with more.

Here are a few tips that will help you improve your relationship with your technician.

Before the tuning:

- Confirm your appointment and make arrangements to be home when they arrive.

- If you need to cancel or reschedule your appointment, let your technician know right away. Don't wait until the night before.

- Respect the business hours of your technician. Avoid texting them on nights and weekends. Don't insist that they come at irregular business hours or weekends to service your piano if their business does not operate during those times. We need days off, too.

- Understand that your emergency is not your technician's emergency. For example, think ahead and schedule a tuning in advance if you have family coming in for the holidays. Every year, I get panicked calls a week or two before Christmas asking if I can fit them in. Those weeks are usually completely booked well in advance.

- Accept any travel fee that may be charged as a result of your location relative to your technician. Their driving time has an opportunity cost.

- Take things off the top of the piano. There is typically no need to move the piano away from the wall.

During the tuning:

- Tell your technician about your piano needs and concerns. If there is something you'd like them to focus on, let them know before they begin.

- Feel free to watch, but don't hover. Every technician will have a different comfort level on this one.

- Don't vacuum or schedule yard maintenance during your tuning time. You'd be surprised how often this happens.
- Some background noise is completely understandable, but any amount of background music makes tuning incredibly difficult.

After the tuning:

- Be open to future-scheduling your next appointment. Just like at the dentist, it can be nice to put your next appointment on both of your calendars before your technician leaves.
- Ask what recommendations they have. For some reason, many technicians will not initiate a discussion about regulation and voicing services, but you know better now. Ask them what else you can do beyond the tuning to improve your instrument.
- Leave a tip. This is optional of course, but as with any other job in the service industry, tips are very much appreciated.
- Tell a friend. For many technicians, word-of-mouth is their primary way of generating business. For some, it is the only method they need.

As you get to know each other, you may soon find yourself discussing non-piano related subjects with your technician; asking after their kids or hobbies. For many technicians, the interaction with people in their homes is one of the highlights of the profession.

Finally, I would like to offer some suggestions on how you can improve the descriptions you provide your technician about any issues your piano may be experiencing.

When describing an issue, include the following:

- **Who** – is making the request
- **What** – are the parts doing
- **When** – does the problem occur
- **Where** – which note
- **Dy** – namic level
- **How Many** – pedals are being used

Who – We service a lot of pianos. Most full-time technicians provide over one thousand tunings per year. Before jumping in and expecting us to remember you and your piano, please provide us with a little bit of information. Things like your name, where you live, the brand of your piano and when we last serviced the instrument.

What – are the parts doing? This information is incredibly helpful. Whenever someone tells me that a key is sticking, I ask, "Is the key visually sticking down?" About half of the time, the answer is "No, the key comes back up, but…" This information helps immensely when trying to diagnose an issue.

When – does the problem occur? If a note is clicking, does that click occur when the hammer hits the string, or when the hammer falls back down? Or perhaps the problem only occurs when the note is repeated quickly.

Where – the note number. Remember the note numbers from Question 8? Allow me to include the same picture again (Figure 14.1) and repeat a few sentences from that question. If you remember nothing else from this book, remember this numbering system. It is *significantly* easier when a pianist tells us that E6 has a particular issue, as opposed to "there is an issue with one of the notes in the area a little bit above middle C, but not quite in the notes on the top of the piano."

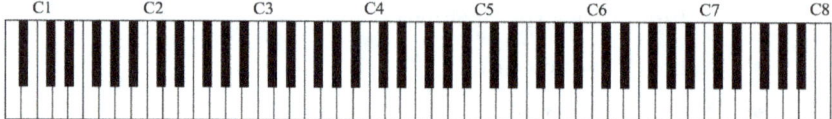

Figure 14.1 – Note numbers on a keyboard.

Dy – namic level. Does the problem only occur when the key is pressed softly? Or only on hard blows? That can be very revealing.

How Many – pedals are being used? Is this problem made worse when the sustain pedal is pressed? Does the shift pedal squeak? Does the sticking damper fall back down when the sostenuto pedal is pressed? Again, the more information you can provide the better.

Let's work through an example. The information added in each step will be in bold. At first, the problem could be any number of things. By the end, I can tell you exactly what issue this piano is having.

Original

- One of the notes on my piano is making a clicking sound. Can we schedule a time for you to come help with this?

Who

- **This is John Smith. You tuned my Kawai grand piano last October.** One of the notes on my piano is making a clicking sound. Can we schedule a time for you to come help with this?

What

- This is John Smith. You tuned my Kawai grand piano last October. One of the notes on my piano is making a clicking sound. **The key plays and returns as expected, as does the hammer and damper.** Can we schedule a time for you to come help with this?

When

- This is John Smith. You tuned my Kawai grand piano last October. One of the notes on my piano is making a clicking sound **the moment the hammer hits the strings**. The key plays and returns as expected, as does the hammer and damper. Can we schedule a time for you to come help with this?

Where

- This is John Smith. You tuned my Kawai grand piano last October. **C3** makes a clicking sound the moment the hammer hits the strings. The key plays and returns as expected, as does the hammer and damper. Can we schedule a time for you to come help with this?

Dy-namics

- This is John Smith. You tuned my Kawai grand piano last October. C3 makes a clicking sound the moment the hammer hits the strings. The key plays and returns as expected, as does the hammer and damper. **The click only occurs on strong forte blows.** Can we schedule a time for you to come help with this?

How Many (Pedals)

- This is John Smith. You tuned my Kawai grand piano last October. C3 makes a clicking sound the moment the hammer hits the strings. The key plays and returns as expected, as does the hammer and damper. The click only occurs on strong forte blows. **It seems to go away when the middle pedal is pressed.** Can we schedule a time for you to come help with this?

When you discover an issue on your piano, be sure to write down as many of these details right away. Don't wait until the technician gets to your piano. Try as you might, you likely won't remember exactly which note it was, only the general area. Just like when you take your car to the mechanic, the problem has a tendency to disappear when the technician arrives to inspect it. Your ability to provide as many details as possible will help your technician address the problems (yes, even the ones that seem to disappear).

Section 3

How do I Purchase a Piano?

Question 15

How Old is My Piano?

I hope you will indulge me in one more analogy to help teach about how pianos age. There is a lot of misconception out there about this. Many people think that pianos are like wines or violins that get richer with age. The reality is that pianos depreciate monetarily much more like cars, and age more like humans. Everything tends to work great in the first few decades of life. As we reach our thirties or forties, everything continues to function, but we can't help but notice that things aren't quite the same as they used to be. In our fifties and sixties, those who took better care of their bodies during decades past fare much better; so too do pianos that were blessed with more routine tuning, regulation and voicing. By the time a piano reaches its seventies or eighties, it's time for some figurative knee or hip replacements (a.k.a. major rebuilding work) if the instrument is to continue to have much musical value.

A good rule of thumb is that the average musical lifespan of a piano is around fifty years. Nearly all pianos continue to be played in people's homes well beyond the fifty-year mark, but the owners of these pianos are rarely naive enough to ignore that their instrument has long since past its prime.

To determine the age of your piano, you must first locate the piano's brand and the serial number. The brand is typically easy to find. It is almost always stamped onto the fallboard and the plate. The serial number can be more elusive. The most common location for a serial number in a grand piano is on the front of the plate. You may need to remove the music desk to find it (Figure 15.1). The most common location for a serial number in an upright piano is on the top of the plate. You will have to open the lid to see this number (Figure 15.2).

Figure 15.1 (Left) – Serial number on a grand piano.

Figure 15.2 (Right) – Serial number on an upright piano.

With this information in hand, you can consult an atlas that lists what serial numbers each piano company produced in each year. If the piano brand is still being manufactured, then the company's website likely has a search function for this. For older pianos, the most comprehensive resource available is the *Pierce Piano Atlas*. Honestly, the easiest thing to do is to send the serial number to your technician and to ask them to look up the year for you. They are familiar with this process and should be able to tell you the age fairly quickly.

Question 16

How Much is My Piano Worth?

Brace yourself. The answer to this question might not be what you want to hear. In my experience, piano owners tend to *significantly* overestimate the value of their instrument. The reality is, your piano is ultimately only worth what someone else is willing to pay for it. Yes, even if it did belong to your grandmother and she was a concert pianist. If you are interested in knowing about how much your piano is worth, then go online and see what a piano similar to yours is selling for. Remember, pianos depreciate more like cars. So again, brace yourself. If you own an older upright piano with beautiful exterior casework, you may be surprised to see pianos similar to yours listed online for $200, or maybe even for free.

Pianos are not financial investments. Tragically, I was once called in to inspect four concert grand pianos that a woman and her husband had been storing for decades because they were under the impression that they would be an excellent financial investment. The husband had recently passed away and I had the unpleasant burden of informing his widow that these pianos that had taken up so much space in their home all these years were simply not worth what she hoped they would be. First of all, not very many places have room for a nine-foot piano, and even if they do, why would they purchase one that was over forty to fifty years old. She claimed that they were "as new" because they were never played. Again, broken-hearted, I explained that while *they* may not have played the pianos, *the seasons* certainly did, year after year, while they never invested in tuning or any other maintenance. I spent two full days cleaning, tuning and regulating these four instruments in a desperate attempt to get them into a condition where they could be sold. I then took pictures and provided her with estimated values. After nearly a year of trying, at my suggestion, she ended up selling the pianos on consignment through a local piano dealer. When all was said and done, this family's investment fared only slightly better than if they had hid the cash under their mattress.

Be wary of any salesperson that encourages you to purchase a piano from them on the grounds of a potential financial investment. They may even show you charts demonstrating how fifty years ago this piano sold new for $10,000, and today it sells new for $90,000. That may be true, but this does not mean that the person who purchased their piano fifty years ago should expect to sell their piano for $90,000. They would likely be happy to get $15,000 for it. Which isn't bad, but certainly not what anyone who can do math would consider a financial investment.

This is not to say that pianos aren't worth investing in, only that the investment shouldn't be seen as financial. Unlike cars, pianos tend to be a one-time purchase that can bless a family for generations. I always encourage people to think long-term, and not to settle when purchasing a piano. I know they can be expensive, but if done right, this is the piano you will cherish into your golden years and pass on to the next generation. Seen in this light, the investment feels less overwhelming. In short, if you choose your love, then you will love your choice every day for the rest of your life.

Sadly, all good things must come to an end. A time will come when the cost of maintaining the family heirloom simply outweighs the value of the instrument. I have shared this moment with countless families. I arrive at the home to find grandma's piano in disrepair. The tuning pins are too loose to hold a tuning, the bridge is cracked, some of the hammers have broken off. I call the family together and explain that I cannot in good conscience charge them for work that I cannot ensure will last—it is no longer worth investing money in this instrument. The money would be far better spent in saving up for a newer instrument. My monologue, which often brings tears to people's eyes, typically sounds something like this:

"I'm not saying you have to get rid of it, but I am saying that this piano has lived its life as a musical instrument. The reality is that your grandmother's legacy is not the piano, but the gift of music in the lives of her children and grandchildren. While this piano will always carry significant sentimental value, at this point, the best way to honor her legacy would actually be to purchase a newer piano so that the gift of music can be provided to generations to come. You have the opportunity to do that for your family legacy and I'd be more than happy to help you navigate that process."

Question 17

Is My Piano Worth Rebuilding?

A friend of mine recently came to me needing some advice. His brother wanted to find a piano for his kids to take lessons on. Online, he saw a spinet piano from the 1950s that a technician had "fully restored." They were only asking for a few thousand dollars and his brother leaped at the opportunity. He was now the proud owner of his very own "fully restored" piano.

Isn't that a lovely story? Well, as you probably have imagined, that is not where this story ended. You see, what was advertised as a great deal was turning out to be nothing more than a great deal of work. When the tuner came to tune the piano, a bass string snapped. A few months later, a few notes stopped working as the rubber grommets on the poor old spinet began to crack and fall off. Then one of the wooden pieces holding a damper cracked and the piano started ringing.

I asked my friend if the sale of the piano came with any sort of warranty. Not surprisingly, the answer was no. His brother had already invested hundreds of dollars into additional work and wanted nothing more than to travel back in time and tell his former self that he was making a mistake.

As it turns out, what the technician had called "fully restored" was nothing more than a set of new hammers and a refinished case. While it looked lovely on the outside, nearly everything on the inside of this piano was over seventy years old. To make matters worse, strictly speaking, the technician didn't do anything wrong. The piano was working fine when it was sold and since piano technology is an unregulated industry, they were free to define "fully restored" as they saw fit. Tragically, my advice was for my friend's brother to stop throwing money at his current piano and to start saving up to purchase something that would meet his family's needs.

Have I scared you yet? Because that was my intention. The decision to purchase a rebuilt piano should not be made causally, and the same could be said about the decision to rebuild your own piano. Carefully selecting a rebuilder is infinitely more important than selecting a technician. If you are unhappy with a tuning, then you may find yourself out a few hundred dollars, but nothing more. Simply have another technician come out and the issues should be resolved. If you are unhappy with a rebuild however, then you are out thousands (if not tens of thousands) of dollars and pressing "control-z" is usually not a realistic option.

It is also important to realize that when you pay for a rebuild, you are buying a piano that you have never played. That should be obvious, but the sentimental component of a rebuild often overshadows this fact. If money isn't an issue, and you don't play seriously, then perhaps this can be overlooked. But if money is tight and you are a serious pianist, then you need to stop and consider this reality very carefully. Are you willing to pay this amount for a piano you have never played?

Fully Rebuilt, Restored, or Refurbished

As mentioned, the problem with terms such as "fully rebuilt," "completely restored," or "newly refurbished" is that they are not defined. In many respects, a rebuild is only as good as what was left undone. Always ask what is included in the price of a rebuild, and perhaps more importantly, what aspects will be left untouched.

To me, a full rebuild of a grand piano would include all of the following:

- New soundboard
- New bridge or bridge cap
- New pinblock
- New strings, agraffes, and tuning pins
- New damper action
- New damper felts
- New hammers
- New action parts that are pinned to the appropriate level of friction
- New key bushings
- New keytops (it is rare for an entire keyboard to be replaced, although it is sometimes necessary)
- The keyboard weighed off for ideal touch
- Full regulation and voicing
- Replacement of pedal felts and leathers
- And while solely aesthetic, a complete refinishing of the case, case parts, and plate.

It is unlikely that a local piano rebuilder will be equipped to provide everything listed above. Often, those seeking a full grand piano rebuild end up shipping their piano out of state. Not surprisingly, this level of rebuild costs quite a bit of money, nearly always in the 5-digit range. Meaning that you could often buy another piano for the cost of the rebuild. That may or may not be your best option, depending on the potential of your piano and the level of sentimental value you feel. Typically, these types of rebuilds are reserved for high-end brands, where the cost of a comparable replacement far exceeds the expensive cost of the rebuild.

As you consider the price, it is important to keep in mind that a full rebuild of this level should provide your piano with an additional 50 years of musical life (much like a new piano), whereas a partial rebuild will likely only allow for an additional decade or two before issues start to creep back in.

This does not mean that a partial rebuild is unacceptable. For example, if your piano is thirty years old and you are a serious player, then a partial rebuild might be exactly what your piano needs to thrive. Regulation and voicing can only access the potential of the parts, and if your hammers have some serious mileage on them, then your piano would likely benefit immensely from new hammers and/or new strings without the need for additional rebuilding at this moment in the piano's life. This would also be an excellent time to rebush the keys and repin the action parts.

While it is important to be wary of people who advertise pianos as "fully restored," or "completely rebuilt," I want to be clear that these are not scams. Very few pianos are deserving of a full rebuild as I have defined it. Each rebuilder must objectively look at the potential of each piano and determine how much rebuilding is warranted, and what is economical within his or her business model. I also don't want anyone to think that they should never purchase a rebuilt piano. It may very well be that doing so is the most cost-effective way to meet your family's musical needs. Just be sure to ask the right questions and to do your homework *before* you make the purchase.

Two Common Alternatives & One Common Oversight

The most expensive things to rebuild are the structural components such as the soundboard and pinblock. Some common alternatives piano rebuilders will employ to make their rebuilds more affordable include restringing a piano with larger tuning pins, and shimming and/or refurbishing the soundboard. Increasing the size of the tuning pins can provide the piano with increased stability without a need to replace the entire pinblock. Shimming any soundboard cracks will return much of the sustain and power lost overtime. These alternatives tend to buy the piano decades of musical life. However, the wood is still old and so these techniques, while economical, are not nearly as beneficial as replacing the pinblock and soundboard.

One common oversight I see from rebuilders is offering to install new hammers on a grand piano without weighing off the keyboard. This isn't a problem if the new hammers weigh the exact same as the original hammers, but that is rarely the case. Think of it like a scale with two sides. The weight of the hammer is on one side, and the weight of the key (and the wippen) is on the other side. These two weights need to balance each other. What often happens is that when the new hammers are installed, they throw off this balance, which dramatically affects the touch of your piano.

If you are getting new hammers, be sure that the keyboard will also be weighed off. Otherwise, the tone of your piano may improve while the touch is made worse. Again, I believe that this is also not a scam, it is usually the result of ignorance on the part of a less-experienced rebuilder.

In short, many grand pianos are worth rebuilding to some extent, especially those where sentimental value is high. If the piano is from a high-end manufacturer, then the cost of a comparable replacement usually far exceeds the cost of a full rebuild. Most upright pianos are not worth rebuilding unless sentimental value is quite high and money isn't an issue. This is because the cost of a comparable replacement may be less than the cost of the rebuild.

Remember this:

1. Selecting a qualified rebuilder is even more important than selecting a qualified technician.
2. When you pay for a rebuild, you are buying a piano that you have never played.
3. A rebuild is only ever as good as what was left undone.

Question 18

Should I Buy New or Used?

By now, I have compared pianos to cars enough times that you might reasonably ask, "Why buy new, when so much value is lost when the car is driven off the lot? Wouldn't it be wiser to purchase a lightly used vehicle?" In theory, yes. If you are lucky enough to find a nice ten to fifteen-year-old piano for sale, then go for it! Although, you should probably factor in the cost of a full regulation and some voicing to your purchase, as the piano is likely overdue for these services.

That said, unlike cars, people rarely trade in a lightly used piano to get the newest model. Pianos tend to be one-time purchases. This means that the used piano market tends to be full of older pianos, leaving the potential buyer with essentially one of two choices: purchase a new piano, or purchase a used piano with a lot of miles on it. Between the two, I strongly encourage people to think long-term and buy new.

Let's say you are in your forties and are looking to purchase a piano for your home. If you buy a new piano, then you can look forward to fifty years of relatively stress-free piano ownership. From now and into your nineties, your piano will likely only need tuning and an occasional regulation and voicing session. While the initial investment was large, the long-term benefits were well deserved and thoroughly enjoyed.

Let's imagine that instead you choose to buy a used piano. Even though the piano is pushing fifty years old, the price is right and the condition overall seems to be in good shape. All is well, until ten years down the road when some keys stop working. You pay to have them fixed and don't think much of it. A few years later, you play on your neighbor's newer piano and are drawn in by the beauty of the instrument. You've never had a musical experience like that with your own piano. You pay your technician to provide some regulation and voicing services. These help some, but you still want a little bit more. You decide you want to invest in new hammers, but never follow through. As you reach retirement age, you briefly humor purchasing a newer piano, but you aren't in love with the idea of getting a different piano so late in life. You decide to make do with what you have. After all, over the years you have found yourself playing less and less. The piano has become more of a piece of furniture than a musical instrument. You know it needs work, but you continue to put it off. Eventually, you downsize and decide to give the piano to one of your kids, but none of them are interested.

I have come across thousands of pianos and piano owners during my career. I have seen both of these scenarios play out countless times. This is why I encourage pianists to think long-term and not to settle. Choose your love and you will love your choice for the rest of your life.

One common situation I find is parents who don't play, but want their children to take lessons. They are extremely reluctant to invest in a piano since they aren't sure if their kids will take a serious interest in it. I completely understand this! However, it is important that these parents realize that the piano they provide their children with will have a measurable impact on the interest they take in their lessons. In my experience, learning to play on a piano you found online for free is a lot like asking your kids to learn how to play basketball in flip-flops. I'm not saying you need to go out and buy your kids a new pair of Air Jordans, but they will enjoy learning the piano significantly more if you could provide them with a decent pair of sneakers. The nicer the piano, the stronger it pulls you in.

Question 19

Should I Buy Acoustic or Digital?

As a piano technician, I realize that my opinion on this subject is incredibly biased. After all, servicing acoustic pianos is my livelihood. Encouraging you to purchase an acoustic piano could be seen as a way of ensuring my job security, but I think there is more to it than that.

A digital piano might be the best fit for your musical needs. In my opinion, a digital piano is often a better choice than a free acoustic piano you found online, especially if that piano is a spinet or an upright grand (more on these later). There is no doubt that the biggest advantage to owning a digital piano is that the maintenance needed for it is next to nothing. Digital pianos do not need to be tuned. When you consider that an acoustic piano requires at least an annual or bi-annual tuning, financially, that alone adds up fairly quickly. However, unlike an acoustic piano that can last fifty plus years, digital pianos, like all technology, will need to be replaced after a period of time. Nicer ones tend to last around ten to fifteen years.

If you do opt for a digital piano, then I strongly encourage you to invest in one with weighted keys, a base with pedals, a full eighty-eight-note keyboard, and other features that more accurately simulate the touch of an acoustic piano. There are even hybrid pianos being made today that have real action parts in them that can be regulated.

Technology is also being incorporated into acoustic pianos in new and exciting ways. Digital player systems are becoming more common, as are silent mode features and MIDI controllers that allow a composer to input data to a computer from an acoustic piano.

At the risk of sounding overly romantic, the pianist ultimately develops a relationship with the piano. The piano draws in the performer and encourages them to create and explore. While digital pianos have improved significantly over the decades, I don't believe that the sampled sounds can ever truly capture the emotion an acoustic piano can communicate. While they are useful tools, I have never heard of someone attending a digital piano recital, and I don't think I ever will.

Question 20

Should I Buy this Piano?

There will come a moment in your life when you need to decide whether or not you should buy a certain piano. This moment is a turning point. The decision you make will affect your family's musical lives for generations. When this moment arrives, I want you to pause and feel the implications of your choice. Don't make this decision casually.

Remember, when it comes to pianos, what at first appears as a great deal, can often end up becoming a great deal of work. The easiest way to spare yourself from grief is to purchase a new piano, but since I can't force you to make that choice, allow me to sum up everything we've learned together in Ten Piano-Purchasing Commandments.

1. Thou shalt not get a free piano.

Trust me, it is free for a reason.

2. Thou shalt not purchase a piano that is over 50 years old.

Send the brand and serial number to your technician to find out the age.

Following this one commandment will likely rule out over 80% of the used piano market.

3. Thou shalt not purchase a spinet piano or an upright grand piano.

The third commandment is related to the second commandment. Spinet pianos are smaller upright pianos, usually only coming up to your waist (Figure 20.1). In this unique design, the wippen does not sit on the back of the key. Instead, they feature what is called a drop action (Figure 20.2). These pianos were incredibly popular during the 1930s and 40s. Most of the "grandma's pianos" out there are spinets. These pianos stopped being produced around the late 1980s. Meaning that the *newest* a spinet can be is close to fifty years old. Most are much older.

Figure 20.1 – Spinet piano.

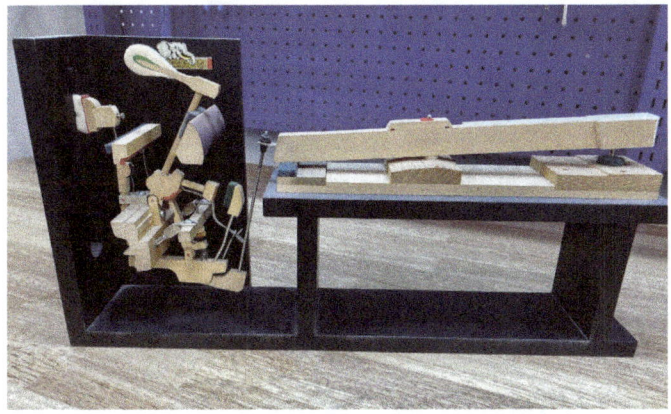

Figure 20.2 – Spinet piano action (notice the piece on the back of the key connecting it to the wippen).

An upright grand is on the opposite end of the height spectrum. These upright pianos are very tall, usually coming up to your shoulder (Figure 20.3). The action on these pianos features a long piece called a sticker that connects the capstan to the wippen (Figure 20.4). These were incredibly popular around the turn of the twentieth century. They were often adorned with breathtaking casework. Don't let the stunning exteriors deceive you; most of these pianos are over one hundred years old.

Figure 20.3 – Upright grand piano.

Figure 20.4 – Upright grand piano action (notice the long wooden piece connecting the back of the key to the wippen).

4. Thou shalt not purchase a piano with a cracked soundboard, bridge, or pinblock.

Cracked soundboards aren't nearly as life-threatening as people often make them out to be. Unless the crack is producing a rattle, many pianos can continue to be played with a cracked soundboard. But this doesn't mean you should buy one with a crack (Figure 20.5)!

Figure 20.5 – Cracked soundboard.

A cracked bridge can make a piano nearly impossible to tune with any level of stability (Figure 20.6); this is a huge red flag.

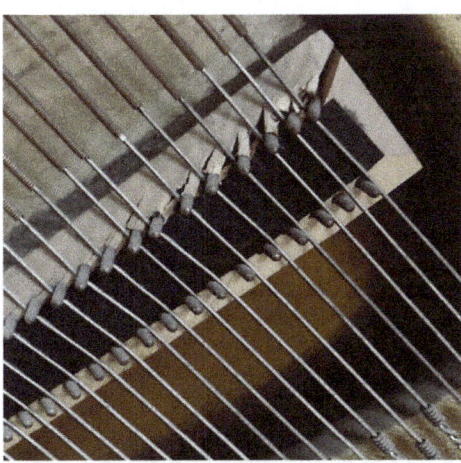

Figure 20.6 – Cracked bridge.

A cracked pinblock is the worst of them all. You can't see the pinblock, but you can usually find a loose tuning pin by playing up and down the keyboard listening for any notes that sound *ridiculously* out of tune (Video 20.1). Like when playing one note sounds like playing a cluster of notes with your fist. That is the sound of a loose tuning pin in a cracked pinblock.

Video 20.1 – Cracked pinblock.

As it turns out, the fourth commandment is also related to the second commandment, since these structural issues typically only occur on pianos over fifty years old.

5. Thou shalt not purchase a piano that hasn't been tuned in recent memory.

Tuning a piano is one of the best ways to uncover hidden issues. If no one remembers the last time the piano was tuned, then it is worth paying a tuner to come tune the piano before you buy it. If they discover that the piano cannot be tuned for whatever reason, then that was money well spent to help you avoid making a decision you'd regret.

6. Thou shalt not purchase a piano that you have never played.

Unless of course, you are paying for your own piano to be rebuilt.

7. Thou shalt, whenever possible, purchase a piano brand that is still being manufactured.

This makes things like ordering replacement parts so much easier.

Additionally, since most US based manufacturers closed their factories around the 1980s, the time is not far distant when the fifty-year rule will apply to all pianos made by these once popular and recognizable brands.

8. Thou shalt always ask what was left undone when considering an instrument advertised as "rebuilt".

A rebuild is only as good as what was left undone.

9. Thou shalt always involve a technician BEFORE you make a purchase.

Far too often, the technician is only brought in after the piano has been moved and the family spends the summer painting the case in their garage! There's more than one thing wrong with this situation.

10. Thou shalt not settle.

Think long-term. Choose your love and you will love your choice every day for the rest of your life.

Conclusion

By this point, you have likely sensed that as a piano technician, I hear certain questions and phrases over and over again. One such phrase is "I wish I hadn't stopped taking lessons as a kid." As we grow up, we seem to find within ourselves a desire to connect to music in deeper, more meaningful ways. There is a peace that comes from ignoring our social media feeds, pausing our Spotify playlists, and sitting down to create and play music. It is exactly that: playing. When we allow our minds to play, we can unplug and ironically, this recharges us. Another thing I hear often is people apologizing for merely playing for their own enjoyment. "Oh, I'm no concert pianist. I just play to relieve stress at the end of the day." Since when did that matter? Why is it that in our society, we seem to have determined that you should be playing in a concert hall or not at all?

Music doesn't care if you are in a concert hall, or in your apartment. Music doesn't care how old you are, or what language you speak. Music doesn't care about the color of your skin, where you grew up, or how much money you have. Try as we might, humans do care about these things, and we can't seem to keep ourselves from caring. Fortunately, music, like all art, transcends us humans.

When was the last time you enjoyed live music?

When was the last time you got goosebumps from listening to music?

When was the last time you gave a *true* standing ovation? Not the obligatory one you give at your child's school concert. I am talking about that moment when the final note is played and you involuntarily leap from your seat. You applaud to become a part of that life-changing moment, to extend it just a little longer, never wanting it to end.

The piano matters because music matters.

Understanding how the piano works matters because the piano is the centerpiece in so many musical settings. There is a piano in every recording studio, jazz club, practice room, and recital hall. There is a piano in nearly every house of worship, and nearly every house on your street. Thus, understanding how the piano works is a step toward understanding the world around us. It's been over three hundred years now since Cristofori invented the piano. Since then, the world has seen the likes of Mozart, Beethoven, Chopin, Rachmaninoff, Liszt, Scott Joplin, Thelonious Monk, Billy Joel, Paul McCartney, Elton John, and you. The piano has changed the world, but it has also changed your life. And that matters, because you matter.

Bonus Question

How Did You Learn How to Do This?

I couldn't walk away from this book without answering the question of where I learned how to work on pianos. This might actually be the question I receive the most often. Many people discover the trade later in life and take it on as a second career. I was fortunate enough to stumble upon it while studying music as an undergraduate student. It was all thanks to the homework assignment that changed my life.

I was in a Music Entrepreneurship class taught by the up-and-coming composer Andrew Maxfield. On the first day of class, he asked us to list five career paths that we thought would be fulfilling (they didn't even necessarily have to be related to music). At the time, I fancied myself an aspiring film composer and so that made the top of my list. I had just taken my first class on audio engineering and loved it, and so recording engineer and broadcast engineer took the second and third slot. I felt pretty good about myself for having an Option A, B, and C, but no one had ever challenged me to come up with Options D and E before, and I was at a loss. What else in this wide universe did I think could be a fulfilling career?

As I sat down with my homework, a pop-up concert was starting in the lobby of the music building. The piano technician came out to help move the piano into place and touch up the tuning. Wanting to finish the assignment, I wrote piano tuner in the fifth and final slot. (I don't remember what I wrote as my fourth option.)

I figured I'd turn in my homework and never think about it again. To my surprise, on the second day of class we were informed that we had the rest of the semester to find and interview someone at least 10 years down each of our five paths. Not knowing any piano tuners, I figured the easiest thing to do would be to email the ones employed by the School of Music. After interviewing Keith Kopp, I was extended an invitation to start coming in to learn how to tune, which eventually led to an apprenticeship in the piano shop. And just like that, my life was changed forever.

Tragically, opportunities to learn piano technology are dwindling along with those of many other trades. I don't have the solution, but

I want to be part of the solution. I am therefore excited to announce a follow-up to this book entitled "How to Work on Pianos: *A Beginner's Course in Piano Tuning and Maintenance.*"

This second book is intended for those who want to see if a career in piano technology is for them. As such, it will ask things that go beyond just reading. For example, you will need access to an upright and grand piano to practice on. You will also need to invest in some basic tools and work through some hands-on homework and online quizzes. By the end, I can't promise that you'll be able to go out and tune pianos for a living, but I can promise that you'll know whether or not you *want* to tune pianos for a living—and that alone is worth discovering. With any luck, this second book could be the homework assignment that changes your life.

Acknowledgements

If this was a typical publication, you might expect to see a bibliography at this point in the book. However, so much of what has been presented here is not written down, as much as it has been passed down. I therefore wish to give credit to my mentors.

I will forever be indebted to Keith Kopp and Jim Busby for taking me under their wings and patiently introducing me to this field.

I am so grateful for Greg Cheng and Bob Parini for always making themselves available to answer my questions without judgment.

I would like to thank Greg Sikora for humbling me by focusing not on my strengths as others had done, but on my weaknesses and how they might be improved.

To Dr. Li Yeoh, thank you for encouraging me to research and write.

To Justin Holcomb, for modeling how to mentor and teach with both passion and compassion.

My deepest gratitude to Rick Baldassin, for seeing in me a lofty potential, then sharing liberally the knowledge and wisdom required to strive for it.

I would also like to recognize my wife Nora and our children, who have supported me every step of our journey together.

Lastly, as a person of faith, it feels appropriate to thank God for guiding me to this fulfilling career and for placing the people listed above in my path.

About the Author

Jason Cassel was born and raised in Southern California and now works as a piano technician for the Brigham Young University School of Music in Provo, Utah (an hour south of Salt Lake City). He received his undergraduate degree from BYU in Commercial Music with an emphasis in Sound Recording. While in school, he worked as a student apprentice in the university piano shop.

After graduating and becoming a Registered Piano Technician, Jason moved to Philadelphia to work for the Steinway and Yamaha dealer in that area. After his first son was born, he decided to attend the Masters of Piano Technology program at Florida State University, the only program of its kind in the country, accepting only two graduate students every two years. He spent the summer between semesters as a senior piano technician for the prestigious Aspen Music Festival & School in Colorado.

He has received the Crowl-Travis Member of Note Award for his contributions to the piano industry, as well as the Jack Greenfield Award in recognition of his nearly three dozen articles in the *Piano Technicians Journal*. Additional publications include an e-book on harpsichord maintenance published by Piano Technician Tutorials, and six instructional video courses on aural tuning available through www.onpitch.com.

Jason is a sought-after instructor at conventions for the Piano Technicians Guild and has presented for Piano Technician's Masterclasses, the North Bennet Street School, the Professional Piano Technicians Network, the Music Teachers National Association, the

Piano Technology School in the United Kingdom, the New Zealand Piano Tuners and Technicians Guild, and the Australasian Piano Tuners and Technicians Association. He is also a featured instructor for the Piano Technicians Academy.

Jason serves as both a Technical and Tuning Examiner for the Piano Technicians Guild and has received manufacturer training from Steinway & Sons, Yamaha, Mason & Hamlin, and Renner USA.

Outside of piano work, Jason enjoys hiking, family bike rides, and playing with his kids. He also loves exploring America's National Parks and has a goal to visit them all! Jason lived in Brazil for two  years as a missionary helping people overcome addictions, strengthen their marriages, and find hope amidst uncertainty and despair. Ele fala Português! He also spent a semester studying the Old and New Testament in the Holy Land.

Jason lives in Utah with his wife and their two sons.

Image of the author in front of the Renner Exhibit at the Musical Instrument Museum (MIM) in Phoenix, Arizona. A bucket-list worthy destination for any music lover.

www.ingramcontent.com/pod-product-compliance
Lightning Source LLC
Chambersburg PA
CBHW061805120626
46550CB00005B/2138